down
to
earth

daikon radish

down to earth

GREAT RECIPES FOR ROOT VEGETABLES

by GEORGEANNE BRENNAN

Photography by SPATHIS & MILLER

CHRONICLE BOOKS
SAN FRANCISCO

Photo styling by Ethel Brennan.
Book and cover design by Sarah Bolles.

Distributed in Canada by Raincoast Books
8680 Cambie Street
Vancouver, B.C. V6P 6M9

10 9 8 7 6 5 4 3 2 1

Chronicle Books
275 Fifth Street
San Francisco, CA 94103

Library of Congress Cataloging-in-Publication Data:

Brennan, Georgeanne, 1943-
    Down to earth : great recipes for root vegetables /
    Georgeanne Brennan ; photographs by Spathis & Miller.
        p.   cm.
    Includes index.
    ISBN 0-8118-0670-7 (pb)
    1. Cookery (Vegetables) 2. Root crops. I. Title.
TX801.B693 1996
641.6'51—dc20   95-48889
                                             CIP

Printed in Hong Kong.

Table of Contents

Acknowledgments

Thanks above all to my husband, Jim Schrupp, for reading, editing, and commenting on the manuscript, for sampling and critiquing all the recipes, for keeping the garden going, and for being a wonderful partner. My appreciation to Charlotte Glenn Kimball and Tom Neeley for responding so quickly to summons for help of all kinds: Rototilling, planting, sampling root dishes, and visionary comments on what goes with what. To Sharon Spain and to my daughter, Ethel Brennan, for bringing their creative energies to recipe testing and development. To Oliver Brennan, Dan and Tom Schrupp, and Robert Wallace for their enthusiastic responses to root dishes of all kinds and for garden help as needed.

A special thanks to my good friend Stuart Dixon of Stone Free Farm in Watsonville, California, who sent me fifty-pound boxes overnight, brimful of the most beautiful organic roots and greens imaginable. They were inspirational. Thank you to Bill Fujimoto, of Monterey Market in Berkeley, California—as in the past, he so generously spent time sharing his knowledge with me. To Bill LeBlond and Leslie Jonath, my editors at Chronicle Books, who are such enthusiasts, remaining encouraging and helpful throughout the process of an idea becoming a book; to Drew Montgomery, the marketing director of Chronicle Books, who first suggested to Bill that I write a book on roots; to my agent, Susan Lescher, a joy to talk and work with; and to Sharon Silva for her insightful and thoughtful editing, as always. Thank you, Ethel, for the perceptive vision and detail you brought to the photo styling, and for ferreting out the best roots possible for cooking and photography; thank you Sharon Spain for cooking to perfection all the food photographed, and to Dimitri Spathis and Michele Miller for their lush photos and their unwavering enthusiasm for this book. Sarah Bolles, thank you for your inventive and inspired design.

To my brother, Sidney

Considered unglamorous, and long associated with poverty and peasantry, roots in fact compose a tremendously versatile and richly flavored group. In purely botanical terms, the root is the part of the plant that anchors or attaches it to the soil and that stores energy for the plant to draw upon during part of its life cycle. Culinarily, though, roots may be thought of as the vegetables we eat that come from underground. Thus, we dine on the swollen stem tips of potatoes, the tightly packed leaves of onions, the corms of water chestnuts, the rhizomes of ginger, and the tubers of yams, as well as the true roots of parsnips and carrots.

This undergound collection exhibits an exuberant range of flavors. Celery root and parsley root are intense, pungent versions of the more familiar celery stalks and parsley leaves. The Allium clan, which includes onions, garlic, shallots, and leeks, are roots not only with a significant sugar content, but also allyl sulfide, the compound that delivers the desirable eye-watering bite. The fierce sting of horseradish, the nutty overtones of Jerusalem artichokes, the haunting oysterlike taste of salsify, and the peppered flavor of radishes also exemplify the distinct tastes discernible among the lowly roots.

Most roots can be eaten raw and while some, like carrots, radishes, and green onions, are common fare, others, such as sweet water chestnuts, mild jicama, aromatic celery root, and nutty Jerusalem artichokes, are less familiar. Shallots, garlic, ginger, and horseradish possess pungent volatile oils and compounds that encourage their use raw as powerful seasoning and flavoring agents.

Some roots, though, are either too strongly flavored to enjoy uncooked—rutabagas, for example—or do not have an appealing taste or texture when raw. Potatoes, sweet potatoes, yams, and taro are hard and unappetizing when raw, but once cooked become soft, and their distinct flavors ascendant.

Root cookery encompasses virtually the entire range of cooking methods, and the roots are perhaps the most multifaceted of all the vegetable types that grace our plates. They can be boiled, steamed, baked, grilled, fried, or roasted. They are suitable for long braising as well as quick stir-frying. They can be cooked whole, grated, chopped, minced, sliced, or diced. Once cooked, they are infinitely adaptable. Savor the thoughts of garlic mashed potatoes, a buttery purée of celery root, a creamy gratin of winter roots and spicy sausage, or luscious dessert flans and soufflés of ginger root or sweet potatoes.

Many of the recipes in this book may be accomplished with roots other than those in their respective ingredient lists, and while in some instances I make specific suggestions, I hope that you will peruse the portraits, both botanical and culinary, in the root notes that follow and, being inspired by the attributes described, create countless variations and adaptations not only of the recipes in this book, but of others as well.

I have chosen to organize the book by subject rather than alphabetically by root. This is because I think roots (along with other vegetables) are traditionally thought of and treated in recipe books as side dishes to meats rather than as fundamental components in everything from salads to sweets, which is how cooks use them today. Today, too, because we are shopping at burgeoning farmers' markets, and have—or would like to have—our own small kitchen gardens, we are cooking seasonally. As seasonal cooks, we need to be able to survey a market stand or our own garden, select what looks best, and then decide how to prepare it. This gives us access to roots in every stage of their growth, so that culinarily we are more versatile. For example, when turnips are tiny and young, you might use them and their greens in salad, lightly steam them with celery root to serve with poached fish, or add them to a spring vegetable ragout. More mature, they might be the star of a gratin, or a primary element with a roast chicken or duck. Put simply, the recipe starts in the garden, not in the book. Roots can be used in so many combinations that an alphabetical listing seemed to shortchange the inherent versatility that is the hallmark of healthful, seasonal cooking.

The chapter called Small Dishes acknowledges the increasing popularity of making a meal of several small plates of equal importance, rather than always choosing a main course accompanied or preceded by dishes accorded lesser importance. The chapter titled Soups and Stews acknowledges that roots are fundamental to these time-honored preparations, and deserve special attention.

This is not meant to be an all-inclusive inventory of root vegetables, of which there are many more than are discussed here. Instead, this is meant to be a comprehensive list of the fresh roots of good quality that are, with a few exceptions, commonly available at farmers' markets, supermarkets, and ethnic and specialty markets.

Additionally, almost all of the roots included, with the exception of the tropicals, can be grown in gardens throughout most regions of the United States. Many are absurdly easy to grow: even the most timid novice will have success with onions, potatoes, radishes, and carrots. Numerous varieties of seeds, root divisions, bulbs, and tubers are available to the home gardener through mail-order catalogs, nurseries, and specialty garden shops. Truly, there is little to compare to the taste of a freshly dug potato with the scent of the earth still in it, or a pulled carrot yet cool from the soil, except perhaps the added thrill that you grew it yourself.

carrots

red beets

Beet
Beta vulgaris

Beets belong to the Chenopodiaceae or goosefoot family, which also includes chard, spinach, and orach. Part root and part swollen stem, the modern beet, of which there are many varieties, descends from selections of the wild beet that grow throughout southern Europe. Shapes may be round and bulbous, flattened, long and pointed, or shaped like a spinning top. The leaves, which are edible, vary among the different varieties and may be deep, dark burgundy; bright apple green veined with scarlet; or a dark pine green with striking red veins.

The intense color of red beets is due to the presence of the pigment betanin, which causes everything touched by the cooked root, including your hands, to become some shade of red. Thus the potato, cream, and cheese of a beet gratin will become a rosy pink, and onions and herrings tossed with beets in a salad will change from white to red.

Not all beets are red. Two notable exceptions are Burpee's Golden Beet, which is a warm yellow with light green leaves veined gold, and the Chioggia beet, which displays concentric red and white rings. Chioggia is an Italian heirloom variety derived from strains planted along the sandy reaches of ground that border the Adriatic Sea, just south of Venice.

In general, red beets have a somewhat stronger and more pronounced flavor than gold or striped beets do, but differences in taste are not exceptional enough to recommend one over the other. The gold and striped beets do not stain and color as the red ones do, however.

Available throughout the year, beets are almost always cooked before eating. To minimize bleeding, the beet must not be cut into before cooking. One inch of the greens is left intact, as is the thin, hairy root tip. Trimming occurs after cooking. Beets can be steamed, boiled, roasted, or parboiled and then grilled. They can be served hot, at room temperature, or chilled, and their juice can be used to make sauces. Good accompaniments include citrus, a plethora of greens, and herbs such as tarragon, chervil, parsley, dill, and fennel. Young, tender beet leaves are delectable raw in salads, steamed, sautéed, or stir-fried, and are often sold on their own, as greens. They are similar in texture and taste to spinach, but have a slightly more pronounced flavor.

A good-quality beet can be identified by a well-formed and scantily haired root. A crooked body, or one that is exceptionally hairy, indicates that the root had to struggle to grow and consequently may be tough. Avoid any root with a dry, scaly brown top as well, as this is a sign that it was partially above ground, exposed to the weather, and now probably tough. Beets should be stored in the refrigerator, as should the greens.

Burdock

Articum lappa

Burdock, a member of the Compositae family, grows wild throughout much of Asia and Europe, and is especially valued in Japan, where it is known as gobo. Perhaps the longest of edible roots, it sometimes reaches four feet in length. The most desirable of these brown-skinned vegetables are very slender, less than an inch in diameter, and perfectly straight.

The aromatic flesh is sweet, a little nutlike, delicate and mild in young roots, stronger in older ones. When preparing the root for cooking, regardless of its age, the skin is just barely scraped away, as much of the flavor is said to be in the flesh closest to the thin layer of skin. Because the flesh browns once it is in contact with air, the skinned root needs to be put immediately into water acidulated with vinegar or lemon juice. If the root is old, it is usually pounded flat with a cleaver before cooking to tenderize it, and even young roots sometimes receive this treatment. Cut into thin slices or julienned, stir-fried, either alone or with carrots, onions, and perhaps beef, and then seasoned with soy sauce is a common treatment. Burdock strips or pieces are also added to soups and to long-cooking stews, where they impart their unusual flavor.

The quality of burdock rapidly deteriorates when it is dried out, and good-quality roots should be very firm and snap when bent. Sometimes they are kept packed in earth to prevent them from drying out, and it is thought that not washing the roots until you are ready to use them will help to retain their moisture and quality. In the home kitchen, store them loosely wrapped in paper, such as a kraft grocery bag. Burdock is generally available year-round.

Carrot

Daucus carota

The carrot, whose origin is in Eurasia, belongs to the Umbelliferae family along with celery root, parsley, parsnip, fennel, and the herbs angelica, cumin, and dill. Although the wild carrot has been known and used since ancient times, it was not until the eighteenth century, after the French seed house of Vilmorin-Andrieux undertook the selection and breeding of carrots for vegetable production, that the fleshy orange root we savor today became the standard. Although most carrot varieties are long and tapered, there are also stocky, broad-shoulder types; round ones; medium-long, blunt-tipped specimens; and short, blunt-tipped or tapered fingerling carrots. In Asia, popular carrot varieties are bright red-orange and up to two feet long, with the roots being no larger across than a generous inch, and in Belgium and Great Britain one still finds the intensely flavored old-fashioned white carrot, a close relative of the wild carrot.

Only in this century has eating raw carrots become common, and today more are eaten raw than cooked. Available year-round, fresh carrots cooked in the most simple ways have a taste of sweet perfume and delicate flavor quite unlike that of a raw carrot, and certainly unlike that of the mush of an overcooked carrot. Raw carrots can be sliced, grated, or eaten whole as is, and their juice can be reduced to flavor stocks, sauces, and vinaigrettes. Carrots may be peeled or left unpeeled. Generally it is a matter of presentation rather than taste, with peeled carrots being more finished and elegant looking, unpeeled appearing more rustic and earthy. In soups and stews where they cook down, the appearance is less significant than in a salad, for example. Because of their pronounced flavor, carrots are an important element in soups, stews, and stocks, where they enhance the overall preparation. When added to roasting meats or vegetables, their natural sugars emerge to glaze and caramelize them during the slow cooking. Good accompaniments to carrots are raisins, dried cherries, dates, coconut, and other members of their family such as celery root, parsley, and dill.

Leafy green tops left on carrots indicate that they have been freshly dug. The tops are edible and may be used as a seasoning. Those sold without their greens attached have generally been in storage. A good-quality carrot of any kind should be firm, dry, and not slippery-skinned, and should not display the green shoulders that signify that they were not grown fully under the ground, and consequently may be bitter.

Celery root, a member of the Umbelliferae family, is a type of celery that forms a large, bulbous swelling where the crown of its root meets the thin, hollow stalks. The root, also known as celeriac, probably has its origin in the bogs and marshes of Eurasia, as does stalk celery, but the starch-storing root celery is much more flavorful than the water-laden stalks

Carrot

Celery Root

Apium graveolens var. rapaceum

of its better-known counterpart. Celery root was selected and developed for cultivation rather late in the history of garden vegetables, and even at the end of the nineteenth century was not commonly grown. In the last one hundred years, the virtues of celery root have recommended it as an outstanding vegetable, and it is now common fare throughout Europe, although it remains a minor vegetable in the United States.

Covered with hairy lumps and whorls and knobs, and with a gaggle of short, gnarled rootlets at its base, celery root is one of the more intimidating root vegetables. Beneath the defensive exterior, though, lies crisp, white flesh whose texture resembles that of the carrot, but has the flavor of amplified celery.

Celery root has a higher water content than the starchier roots of potatoes and parsnip, but unlike them, is delicious raw. It must be peeled first, though, whether it is to be eaten raw or cooked. The stalks and leaves can be used for seasoning, but are generally too fibrous and tough to be eaten raw. Once peeled and shredded, chopped, minced, shaved, or grated, celery root adds a fresh and distinctive taste to salad greens of all kinds. It has an equal affinity for apples, dry cheeses, and fresh green herbs such as tarragon, chervil, chive, and parsley. Celery root may be baked in gratins alone or in combination with other vegetables (puréed celery root and potato is one of the great dishes of the root world). When cubed and steamed with herbed or citrus butter, it is an especially fine companion to roast chicken or game hens.

The best celery root feels heavy in the hand, indicating it is dense and solid, not pithy. The attached stalks should be crisp, not limp and dry, and show green, not yellowing leaves. Celery root is most commonly associated with fall, but it is available year-round. Store the celery root in the refrigerator.

Chervil Root

Anthriscus ceretolium

Chervil root, like leafy chervil, parsley, dill, carrot, and celery, belongs to the Umbelliferae family, but it is considerably more obscure than its kin. Possessing the look of a young, broad-shouldered, pointed-tipped carrot, between four and six inches long, chervil root has dark grayish skin, which is peeled before using, and pale yellow-orange flesh. Also known as turnip-rooted chervil and tuberous chervil, it is native to Europe, and once was as common there as the leafy herb chervil is today. It is now considered to be among the forgotten vegetables, which is unfortunate because it has a fine flesh and delicate flavor.

I had the pleasure of eating chervil root when I was the guest of a professor of agriculture at a university near Angers, France. His particular interest was in the commercial potential of vegetables that had once been popular but were no longer cultivated on a significant scale, and chervil root topped his list as a candidate for contemporary success. He was working in conjunction with a restaurant in Angers whose chef prepared the vegetables brought to him from the university's plot of "forgotten vegetables," and we of course went to this restaurant for lunch. I was served, among other things, a fish from the nearby Loire accompanied with a creamy chervil root purée. It was a soft swirl that resembled *pommes purées,* but the color was a delicate shade of yellow-orange. The texture was light and airy yet substantial, and the flavor was the faint lemon licorice characteristic of chervil.

Although chervil root is not widely available, it does have a future, and should you be so fortunate as to find one in your market, a quality specimen will be firm and solid feeling and should be stored in the refrigerator. Chervil root is most likely to be found in late spring or early summer.

Chicory, a member of the Compositae or sunflower family, is native to Europe, where the readily identifiable bright blue flowers of wild chicory plants can be seen along roadsides and in fields spring through summer. Chicory root is related to leafy endive, radicchio, and escarole and to the other numerous chicories especially prevalent in Italy. Its leaves also share the characteristic bitter taste for which chicories are prized.

At least two chicories are grown primarily for the roots. The most common is the variety called Madgeburg, which is grown to produce coffee chicory. The root is cut into slices, then roasted and ground either to add to coffee or to be used as a substitute for coffee. This is generally produced in Europe, but during World War II hundreds of acres of California cropland were planted to chicory in an effort to augment the coffee rations.

In Italy, a variety called Chivara is cultivated, not for roasting and grinding, but to be sautéed in olive oil, simmered in cream, or steamed and then dressed with oil and vinegar. The flavor is nutty, somewhat like a Jerusalem artichoke, but the texture is considerably more dense and solid. Chicory roots are seasonal, appearing in late fall and winter. In appearance they resemble narrow-shouldered parsnips, about seven or eight inches long, and have pale beige skin that is peeled before cooking.

The leaves of the chicory root, which are large, dark green, floppy, furry, and bitter when mature, are much milder when young. They may be cooked and treated as you would spinach or other greens, or when very young make a powerful addition to a mixed salad of dandelion and other sharp-flavored greens. Chicory roots should be firm, not limp and bendable. Store them in the refrigerator.

Chinese Artichoke

Stachys affinis

A member of the Labiatae or mint family, the Chinese artichoke, although native to China, is not an artichoke at all. It is a small, slim, curly, one- to two-inch-long tuber. Its shape has been compared to that of the Michelin man—layer upon layer of tire rounds. The skin is pale brown and once scrubbed away (peeling is difficult because of the small size and convoluted shape) leaves the tuber almost opalescent. It was introduced into France from Beijing in the late eighteen hundreds, and, not long after, the *Crosnes* or *Crosnes du Japon*—the name comes from one of the locations in France where the tuber was first grown—became a popular novelty. The plant is similar to mint, but produces tubers that are harvested in fall. The stems, roots, and leaves are discarded. In France today, however, these tubers are not as common as they once were, although they can still be found in specialty markets, generally displayed heaped in baskets. Seed tubers, too, are offered for sale to home gardeners, as they are in the United States.

In Japan and China, though, the Chinese artichoke continues to be cultivated and is used to make pickles and as an ingredient in stir-fries and soups. The most customary French treatment is turning the barely cooked tubers in butter and cream, or in the juices of a well-seasoned roast, as small pastas are. Both treatments heighten the delicate flavor of this unusual vegetable. With its slight taste of artichoke and light, white crunchy flesh, Chinese artichokes, like water chestnuts, are toothsome raw in salads.

A good-quality specimen will be firm and without signs of decay. Store in the refrigerator.

Garlic

Allium sativum

Garlic, the most pungent member of the Amaryllidaceae or Amaryllis family, probably originated in Asia, and today is used worldwide. A garlic head or bulb is actually composed of many little bulbs or cloves, each with a bud inside. Sometimes when you cut through or peel back a garlic clove, you discover a green shoot in the middle, the sprouting bud.

As many as three hundred different garlic varieties are in cultivation in various parts of the world, but in the United States one generally sees only three or four kinds: White California, Red Mexican, Pink Mexican, and elephant garlic. The former range from the size of a lime to that of a lemon, but elephant garlic is commonly as large as an orange and is milder than the others. Although there is some difference in the varietal flavor of garlic, of more concern to the average cook is age. As garlic ages and the cloves wither, they become chewy, bitter, and mustily pungent. Fresh garlic is juicy and the flavor round with garlickyness.

The most common way garlic is used is broken into cloves, peeled, and added either raw or cooked as a seasoning. But whole heads of garlic, roasted, baked, or grilled until the meat inside the cloves becomes soft and creamy, figure high on the list for garlic lovers. The flavor remains but the pungency is attenuated during cooking, as the volatile oils responsible for garlic's bite become dissipated and diminished.

Garlic may be used in all stages of its growth, too, not only as mature heads. Green garlic, the first tender shoots from the growing clove, looks like green onions and may be used in much the same way. Baby garlic, the stage of growth when a bulb has formed but the cloves or bulblets inside are immature, resembles small, fresh bulbing or spring onions, and may be used in the same way: baked, boiled, grilled, pickled. In Italy and France in May and June, fresh garlic is sold. Fully formed, the head is surrounded by skin that is not yet dry and papery, but instead still moist and supple. The stalk is firm and green and the flavor is pronounced and sprightly. Garlic flowers and flower buds are edible, and have a delicate taste of garlic that is especially good as a garnish, fresh or deep-fried.

Regardless of variety, garlic heads should be solid and firm and the paperlike skin snugly attached. If, when pressing on the cloves, you find air pockets, or meet with no resistance, the garlic is too old and has started to deteriorate.

Although garlic is available year-round, the new crop starts to appear in July. Garlic is best stored in a dry location, not in the refrigerator. Green garlic, baby garlic, and fresh garlic should be refrigerated, however.

Horseradish

Armoracia rusticana

A native of Europe and Asia belonging to the Cruciferae or cabbage family, horseradish displays dingy, arm-thick hairy roots eight to ten inches long topped with a stubble of green that does not encourage sampling. But the intrepid cook will discover that beneath the scary exterior there is white, super-pungent flesh that makes a superb and versatile condiment. At first slice, the assault on your senses begins. Acrid oils are released that sting your eyes and soar through your head igniting every sinus cavity. Your taste buds experience not only the intensity of the root's mustardlike oils, but also its rough texture and the heat of its high spice flavor.

Horseradish complements beets, turnips, oysters, roast beef, corned beef, salmon, and veal ribs, among other meats and vegetables. Peeled and grated, the raw power of the root may be sampled straight or mixed with cream, milk, mustard, or mayonaise to make a sauce. It can also be combined with other ingredients and used as a seasoning in the same way one uses grated onion.

Handle fresh horseradish as if it were hot chilies or potent onions, wearing rubber gloves when handling the roots, especially if you have sensitive skin, and don't rub your eyes! The volatile oils that are responsible for the taste and the sting diminish rapidly, so for maximum effect serve a preparation using horseradish as soon as possible.

A seasonal root, horseradish is harvested in fall and sold from then through late spring. It stores well in the refrigerator, left unpeeled.

Jerusalem Artichoke

Helianthus tuberosus

Native to North America and members of the sunflower tribe of the Compositae family, Jerusalem artichokes are not artichokes at all. Instead they are tubers that resemble knobby, roundish potatoes. During their growth period, the tubers put forth tall—up to fifteen feet— stalks topped with small sunflowers, hence the tuber's Italian name, edible sunflower, or *girasole articiocco*, which does sound a little like Jerusalem artichoke, and is thought to be the source of the vegetable's nondescriptive name. Sunchoke and *topaimbour* are other common names.

Jerusalem artichokes were introduced into Europe in the sixteen hundreds, and into Asia shortly thereafter. No doubt because they grow so readily in even the poorest of ground and with little care, the tubers became a significant food for animals as well as people. I first grew Jerusalem artichokes not to eat, but because I wanted an instant screen between my house and the neighbor's. I planted them in a row in March, and by mid-June I could no longer see the neighbor's house! In the fall at the end of the season, we cut down the towering flower stalks and dug up bucketfuls of the new tubers. We sautéed them in butter, mashed them like potatoes, and thinly sliced them for salads, and I still gave away lots to friends.

The nutty flavor of Jerusalem artichokes is distinctive but not overbearing. Their skin is thin, but because of the knobs and bumps, they can be tedious to peel. The flesh has a crunchy, firm texture like that of fresh water chestnuts and jicama, and can be used culinarily in the same ways. Since they have a rather high starch content relative to their water content, they mash, purée, and thicken just as other starchy vegetables (potatoes, parsnips) do. Jerusalem artichokes do discolor, staining pink on contact with air, and once peeled should be kept in acidulated water until ready to use. Like artichokes, they will turn black if they are cooked in an iron, aluminum, or other reactive pan.

Seasonal roots, Jerusalem artichokes are available from fall through winter and into late spring. Look for firm ones with the buff-brown or red skin intact. Store them in the refrigerator.

Jicama, a member of the Leguminosae family, is native to tropical America, where the round, flat-topped, pointed root tuber is a cooking staple. It ranges from the size of a grapefruit to that of a cantaloupe. Peel away its thick, pale brown skin to discover the crisp, ivory-colored, slightly bland flesh that tastes both starchy and sweet. Somewhat similar in texture and taste to fresh water chestnuts, jicama, also known as Mexican potato, goes well with a number of fruits and vegetables.

Usually served raw in cubes or slices, jicama can also be eaten lightly cooked, added to a soup or stew as the dish finishes cooking, or used in stir-fries as one would use water chestnuts. Limes, oranges, melons, cheeses, mint, cilantro, arugula, chilies, and tropical fruits such as papayas, mangoes, and pineapples are all good choices to combine with jicama. I like to eat it Mexican-beach style: slices of jicama drizzled first with lime juice, then sprinkled with chili, a little crumbled queso fresco, and chopped cilantro.

A good-quality jicama should be firm, unblemished, and without signs of the grayish mold that appears around the top when the tuber is old and starting to deteriorate. Store in the refrigerator or in a cool, dry place.

Leek

Allium ampeloprasum, Porrum Group

A Mediterranean native, leeks, which are not true roots but tightly folded fleshy leaves, belong to the Amaryllidaceae or Amaryllis family. Their bases, which are blanched by mounding soil around them as the leeks grow, are the primary culinary part of this vegetable. The green part of the leaves closest to the white are usually tender but stronger in flavor than the white part, while the dark green uppermost part of the leaves, good for flavoring broths, is generally too fibrous for eating.

Leeks can be sizable, up to two feet long. Some varieties may grow to be as thick as a fist, while others remain svelte, less than an inch in diameter. Baby leeks are any variety that has been harvested very young, before fully maturing. When tiny—only two or three inches long—they are so delicately flavored and mild that they can be used raw, either whole in salads or as one would chives. Generally though, baby leeks are harvested when they are no thicker than a delicate little finger and six to eight inches long.

Both large and baby-sized leeks can be prepared in a number of ways, and while sometimes used raw, they are more commonly cooked. They may be steamed, grilled, roasted, parboiled, and gratinéed; baked into breads; used in soups and stews; deep-fried; and made into confits. Generally, leeks demonstrate the versatility of onions and can be used in much the same way. Before using, be sure to wash them well, separating the layers of leaves, or even partially slitting the stalks open, to flush out the dirt and sand that so often gets caught within.

A good-quality leek will be firm, not limp. If a leek feels hard and is not pliable, it may be because the seed stalk has begun to develop. The flesh inside will have become a hard, nearly inedible core, and the leek will be good only for flavoring. Store leeks in the refrigerator.

Lotus Root

Nelumbo nucifera

Lotus root, which belongs to the Nymphaceae family, originated in Asia, where it has been cultivated as a pond plant for over three thousand years. Not only is the root—actually a rhizome—eaten, but so too are the bud, seeds, flowers, and leaves. The rhizome has a curious appearance, looking like so many smooth-skinned, buff-colored sausage links, each about two inches in diameter and several inches long, in a chain of three or four. When sliced crosswise into segments, the delicate, lacy flower pattern created by the air passages that extend the length of the root are revealed, making it especially appealing to use the roots sliced in soups or salads where they can be visually as well as culinarily appreciated. Lotus roots are not eaten raw, however; they are blanched or parboiled before adding them to a salad or simply dressing with rice wine vinegar as one might cucumber slices.

The texture of lotus root is crisp and crunchy, and like other mild, somewhat bland roots, it absorbs flavors rather than dominates them. After first being peeled, the roots can be cooked in numerous ways, from steamed to stir-fried. When choosing them, look for those that are sleek and smooth, of a golden buff color rather than a darkish yellow, and free of dark blotches. Store in the refrigerator.

Onions belong to the Amaryllidaceae or Amaryllis family, as do garlic, shallots, and leeks. Composed of layers of modified leaves surrounding a core stem, onions apparently originated in Asia, but have since spread throughout the world, where they have been adapted culinarily by virtually every culture. Round, torpedo, flat-topped, red, yellow, brown, white, small to huge, fresh and storage onions—the variety is impressive and the uses in cooking equally so.

Onion

Allium cepa

These highly versatile roots may be used as a seasoning or a main ingredient. Both pungent and sweet, the extent or dominance of either quality depends largely upon whether the onions are used cooked or raw. Allyl sulfide is responsible for the pungency, which is powerful in the raw onion but virtually disappears during cooking, and the sweetness derives from the onion's high sugar content. Raw onions are generally used in small quantities as seasonings and condiments, sliced onto hamburgers and sandwiches, minced and scattered into salads and salad dressings, mixed into steak tartare, rolled up in tacos, sprinkled on hot dogs, and stirred into salsas. Raw onion sprouts, still topped with their tiny black seed coats, are piled onto sandwiches and folded into green salads, potato salads, and even fruit salads. But it is in cooking that onions come into their glory.

Onions can be grilled or broiled in slices, their sweetness apparent, their pungency attenuated a little but not completely gone. They can be sautéed, stir-fried, deep-fried, baked, or roasted. When slowly cooked, their essence is reduced to a caramelized spread of exquisite sweetness. When made into soup or stuffed, they become the central feature, but it is their ubiquitous presence elsewhere as an ingredient, large or small, from minestrone to scrambled eggs to onion rings, that makes them indispensable.

Onion

The bulb or globe onions, as opposed to green onions (scallions), belong in two general categories: the storage onions of the fall and winter and the sweet onions of spring and summer. The storage onions, most commonly the white or yellow ones, usually have thick, tight skins and dense, strong flesh. They are wonderful for long, slow cooking, as they sweeten delectably without losing their character. When eaten raw, they are hot and spicy. Sweet onions have a milder taste when raw than storage onions, but render less sweetness over long cooking, during which they tend to dissolve. They are superb when grilled, however. The most common sweet onions are the red ones. These onions are often large, two pounds or more, and can be cut into plate-sized slices. White onions and yellow onions, as well as red ones, are often sold fresh, that is, with their greens attached and before they are fully matured and the papery outer skins developed and cured. They are often called spring or fresh onions in the marketplace and the bulb may be anywhere from golf-ball to grapefruit size, and will vary in pungency according to the variety.

A good-quality dry globe onion of any type should be firm and feel heavy in the hand. If the onion shows a green spout, its edible quality has deteriorated. Onions can be stored in the refrigerator, which helps a little to reduce tearing when the onion is cut, or they can be stored in a dry, preferably cool location. Spring or fresh onions should show glistening fresh skin and bright greens. These should be stored in the refrigerator.

Green Onion

A. cepa, A. fistulosum

Green onions, often called scallions, are the immature green stalks of a bulb onion of any kind or color. The stage of immaturity at which the green onion is harvested depends upon cultural and culinary preference. In Japan and China, long, thin, white-shanked ones are the norm, while in England and France, a small swelling at the base of the stalk is common. When the bulb is larger, the immature onion is more often called a spring or fresh onion. The green onions, regardless of variety, are generally milder than fresh or mature bulb onions and are commonly eaten raw, the leafy green as well as the white base. They may also be cooked, and are particularly good grilled or stir-fried.

Like the bulb onion, the Japanese bunching onion, also known as the Welsh onion, originated in Asia, where it remains of preeminent importance. Varieties have been developed for leafiness and length of shank and stem—many types are up to two feet long—as well as for specific growing and harvesting techniques. Used in every stage of growth, the bunching onion is eaten raw, cooked, and dried in long strands. It resembles an immature bulb onion in appearance, but has longer, flapping leaves more akin to those of a leek. Culinarily, treat it as you would any green onion.

The true pearl onion is different from the tiny globe onions commonly marketed as pearl or pickling onions. It is composed of a single layer of flesh, much like garlic, with the interior surrounded by paperlike scales, and it is not readily available. Tiny onions can be blanched to facilitate peeling.

A member of the Umbelliferae family and native to Eurasia, parsnip once dominated Europe as the primary starch vegetable, but in the seventeenth century it was replaced by the potato, a newcomer from the Americas. Cream colored and with broad shoulders that quickly taper down to a thin root tip, parsnips range from five to ten inches long, with the smaller ones generally more tender. They are typified by their very dense, quite sweet, faintly nutty taste that develops when the root, still in the ground, is subjected to freezing temperatures.

Parsnips are a wonderful source of culinary inspiration for me. They can be steamed, boiled, broiled, roasted, braised, or fried. When they are to be part of a final presentation, the skin should be peeled, but if they are going to be part of flavoring a broth or cooked down into a sauce, they can be left unpeeled. Roasted in an oven, they become crisp on the outside and stay creamy sweet inside. Slowly cooked in stew, they dissolve to thicken and sweeten the sauce discreetly. When puréed and seasoned with a little garlic or bits of crispy duck skin, they make you wonder why the parsnip was abandoned in favor of the potato. It couldn't have been taste.

Parsnips are in their prime from fall through early spring, and you will notice that when the first parsnips of the fall appear in the market, they may have a leaf or two attached. But by the following spring, there will not only be no leaves, but perhaps a half inch of the crown will

Japanese Bunching Onion

A. fistulosum

Pearl Onion

A. cepa, Aggregatum Group

Parsnip

Pastinaca sativa

be gone, as the parsnips are increasingly trimmed as they emerge from storage. Store parsnips in the refrigerator.

Parsley Root
Petroselinum sativum var. tuberosum

Parsley, a native of the Mediterranean region, where it still grows wild, belongs to the Umbelliferae family. Generally, parsley is thought of in terms of its leaves and their use as a seasoning or garnish, or for salads. One type of parsley has been selected instead for its short, fleshy root, however. Small (often only three or four inches long) and creamy white, the heavily haired parsley root is tapered but slim, and also goes by the names Hamburg parsley and turnip-rooted parsley. I find its pungent flavor intensely appealing, and as with celery root and carrots, whose texture it resembles, parsley root can be eaten raw, but it is also stellar when cooked, in the same way as potatoes and parsnips. Like the roots whose characteristics it shares, parsley root may be added to warm or chilled salads, used to heighten the flavor of soups and stews, steamed, deep-fried, or sautéed on its own or with other roots.

A seasonal root, look for it from late fall through spring, choosing specimens that are firm, rather than limp. The leaves may still be attached, and these too may be used, but be forewarned that they are more fibrous than those of leaf parsley. Store in the refrigerator.

Potato
Solanum tuberosum

Along with tomatoes, eggplants, and peppers, potatoes belong to the Solanaceae or nightshade family and are native to the New World. Their origin is thought to lie in the Andes mountains of Peru, where the abundant wild potatoes have been dug for centuries by the indigenous Indians. Evidence indicates, too, that several types of potatoes were domesticated there over two thousand years ago, well before the Europeans brought potato tubers back to the Old World. The potato, although known to Europeans by the middle of the sixteenth century, did not become popular or widely planted until the seventeen hundreds. Once it was accepted, though, new varieties quickly became available.

Potatoes, sometimes called white or Irish potatoes to distinguish them from sweet potatoes, are quite varied in their appearance and flavors. Prominent forms are round, kidney- or crescent-shaped, olive or oblong. They may be smooth or knobby, slightly bumpy, deeply or faintly indented. With skins of pale yellow, red, beige, dark brown, ivory, and dark violet, and flesh from starkest white to pale blue or yellow, even with shocking purple or cream streaked with rose available, the potato world exhibits a rich variety of color. Flavors range from butter-sweet to starchy.

Some potato varieties can be stored for long periods successfully. These storage or keeper potatoes are dug at maturity, then cured and stored in special facilities that maintain even temperature and humidity levels. In the United States, these are the thick-skinned types such as the popular Russet. Other potatoes are considered fresh market potatoes, as they do not store well. These go to market when they are dug, and they may be kept for a short period of time.

Any kind of potato can be a new potato, as those are the first ones large enough to be dug and eaten. Unfortunately, most of the potatoes readily available to us—Russet, Red Rose, White Rose, Red Pontiac, and Kennebec—are a scanty representation of the diversity of potatodom. At farmers' markets and specialty stores one can find such potatoes as Ruby Crescent and Yellow Finnish fingerlings and Yukon Golds, all of which are waxy, thin-skinned types, with the latter two being very buttery. Peruvian Purple and All-Blue potatoes, both of which are starchy, are found at these same sources.

Potatoes are not eaten raw, but they may be cooked in almost every way: steamed, boiled, baked, fried, sautéed, even grilled or broiled if parboiled first. Thin-skinned potatoes may be cooked peeled or unpeeled, the choice being aesthetic, or based on the fact that much of the potato's desirable nutrients are found in the skin. Generally, if the dish is a rustic one, consider leaving the potatoes unpeeled, but if it is to be a more elegant presentation, you may want to peel them. Thick-skinned potatoes are usually either peeled after cooking or, if baked, served with the skin intact.

Whenever possible, choose potatoes according to their destined use. For example, potatoes with a high starch content, such as the Russet, are good bakers, as they crumble and flake when baked but will dissolve when boiled. Red Rose and Pontiac are good boilers, as are the waxy potatoes; they hold their shape during cooking and can then be sliced or cubed.

In selecting potatoes, be sure to avoid those with greening skin. As the skin is exposed to light, it begins to turn green and a toxin is created during the process. Sprouts contain the same toxin and should be removed. Potatoes should be stored away from the light, with the keeper potatoes kept in a dry, cool location; the thinner-skinned potatoes are best stored refrigerated.

Radish

Raphanus sativus

The radish, which originated in Eurasia, belongs to the Cruciferae or cabbage family and, along with other members such as mustard and horseradish, contains mustard oil, the source of its hot taste. Radishes fall into two general categories, those that must be grown quickly to ensure crispness and that become pithy and go to seed rapidly, and the hard-skinned winter or autumn radishes. The small round or olive-shaped types, which are red, white, red and white, or some variation tinged with pink or purple, are the quick-grown types. Sometimes referred to as spring radishes, they are almost always eaten raw, so that their peppery crispness can best be savored, and are available year-round. The winter types, which require a longer growing season, are much larger and have thick skins that may need to be peeled before eating. They may be eaten raw, but are frequently cooked.

In northern and eastern Europe, a longtime staple has been the winter or black radish, available from fall through late spring. In cooking, these can be treated as one would a turnip or rutabaga, although the flavor is more pronounced. Consider a few chunks or slices strategically placed to soak up the juices of a piece of roasting pork or a beef shank. Grate them raw to use as you would horseradish, or mix them with butter or cheese for a spread.

Daikon radishes, also known as white Asian radishes, are available year-round and sometimes grow to twenty and more pounds. Here we generally see the smaller forms, which are four to six inches wide, one to two feet long, and up to five inches in diameter. They can be eaten raw, but are also a significant cooked vegetable and are often a major ingredient in soups, stir-fries, and braises, where their pungency mellows and contributes flavor to the dish. These radishes are often pickled for serving as a condiment. Generally they are peeled before using. Fall and winter Asian radishes, also called colored types, are available from fall through late spring and may be mild or hot. They have bright rose or lime green flesh, white skin splashed with green or red around the shoulders, and may be used raw or cooked. These are larger, too, than the familiar round red radishes, being ten to twelve inches long and from two to four inches in diameter.

The young leaves of radishes of all kinds are tender and nicely peppery—a bit like cress. They give a surprise taste to soups and stews, stirred in just before serving, and, of course, are ideal additions to salads. Radish sprouts, which can be purchased or easily grown at home, are yet more tender versions of the leaves and may be used in the same way. The green seedpods of radishes make unusual and flavorful additions to stir-fries. They resemble sugar snap peas in size and shape, but have the sharp taste of radish.

Whatever the variety, radish roots should be firm and turgid, not limp and bendable, and the leaves, if still attached, should be a bright green, not yellowing. Store radishes in the refrigerator.

Rutabagas, sometimes called swedes or Swedish turnips, belong to the Cruciferae family along with other brassicas such as cabbages, cauliflower, and turnips. The rutabaga has been known since the Middle Ages as a garden vegetable and is thought to have been the result of crossbreeding between a turnip and a cabbage—not a very illustrious lineage. In fact, in some areas, rutabagas are considered fit only for animal feed.

Shaped like a clumsy turnip, the rutabaga's flesh and skin are golden yellow, whereas those of the turnip are white, although both may show purple streaking on the uppermost portion of the skin. Rutabaga is potent and if simply cooked on its own, may be too potent. I know this from experience, as I once made a rutabaga soup using a recipe I discovered in a nineteenth-century cookbook. The soup was so strong, so powerful, so impossible to eat, the only thing I could think of to do with it was to bury it in the backyard. But a rutabaga, properly treated, has a distinctive flavor that creates a complexity of taste, particularly when used in combination with milder, sweeter roots such as potatoes or parsnips, with grains, or with sturdy greens.

These old-fashioned roots are eaten cooked, and are suitable for mashing, puréeing, roasting, or deep-frying as one would potatoes. They truly come into their own when assembled around a piece of roasting meat, cooking along in the juices, or when added to a soup or stew.

Rutabagas can be found almost year-round, but with some difficulty in the summer months. They should be firm, not soft or showing mold, and they are best stored in the refrigerator.

Salsify and scorzonera, both natives of Europe and members of the chicory tribe of the Compositae family, are virtually identical in taste and culinary use, their main difference being that salsify has pale tan skin and scorzonera's is black. In both cases, the foot-long, cylindrical roots are only a scant inch in diameter, and, when growing, produce long, narrow spiky leaves and bright purple flowers that open briefly in the morning, then close.

Radish

Rutabaga
Brassica napus, Napobrassica Group

Salsify
Tragopogon porrifolius

Scorzonera
Scorzonera hispanica

The delicate, creamy white, faintly oyster-flavored flesh of the salsify gives it its other popular names, oyster plant and vegetable oyster. (The scorzonera is known as the black oyster plant or black salsify.) The root has the slightly firm yet yielding texture of perfectly cooked young turnips or celery root. Salsify may be steamed and eaten as is—hot, at room temperature, or chilled—or sauced with herbs and butter or a vinaigrette. It may also be fried, napped in a cream sauce and gratinéed, puréed, or used in combination with other root vegetables, all of which allow savoring of salsify's unusual flavor.

The roots must be peeled before cooking. The skin contains a sticky, latex-like substance that will become gummy on your hands, but which is easily removed with a mixture of vinegar and salt. The root discolors when exposed to air, so once peeled, put it in water acidulated with lemon juice or vinegar.

Quite hardy, salsify roots can be left in the ground over winter, or they can be dug and stored in sand-and-earthen trenches or in more modern humidity-and-temperature-controlled facilities. The young, pale shoots that appear during storage may be used in salads or cooked, as can the early shoots that poke through when the seeds are first planted. Wild salsify greens, like purslane and dandelion greens, are a component in gathered salads.

Salsify is a seasonal vegetable appearing from late summer, when it is first harvested, to the end of its storage period in late spring. Most salsify is grown in Europe and imported to the United States, but in green markets, particularly those in the east, locally grown salsify is available. Imported or local, black or cream colored, the roots should be firm, and any leaves or leaf shoots left on the top should be green and without signs of decay. Store in the refrigerator.

Shallot

Allium cepa, Aggregatum Group

Papery-skinned shallots, which are probably of Asian origin, belong to the Amaryllidaceae, or Amaryllis, family. Although we generally eat the mature bulb, the green shoots of young shallots, like those of young garlic, can be eaten, as can the buds and flowers. Numerous shallot varieties are cultivated, and although the large reddish- or brown-skinned types are often preferred for ease of peeling, the small, tight-skinned gray shallots have a finer, more delicate flavor.

Shallots are planted in late winter or early spring, depending upon the region, and harvested in mid- to late summer. In Europe, where the majority of the shallots are grown, tons and tons of the bulbs are sent upon harvest to specialized temperature-and-humidity-controlled bulb storage facilities in Holland, from where they are shipped around the world over the next ten to twelve months. There is generally a short supply of shallots in June and July, however, when the previous year's supply is depleted or of declining quality, and the new crop has not yet been harvested.

Certain shallot varieties that have reddish yellow skins look almost identical to multiplier onions, which, like shallots, produce several clumps of bulbs from a single one. But one taste will tell you whether you have an onion or a shallot, as the subtle flavor of the shallot cannot be confused with the onion's bite.

Like garlic, shallots are most commonly used as a flavoring element in combination with other ingredients rather than as a primary ingredient. In French cooking they hold a singular place, as they are indispensable in such classic sauces as beurre blanc, sauce marchand, and sauce bordelaise. Minced shallots are a common ingredient in vinaigrettes, and they are used whenever a mild expression of the pungent allyl sulfide is wanted to flavor a dish, in a delicate omelet of asparagus tips, for example. Whole shallots should be considered for cooking as well, however. They caramelize beautifully to a rich sweet brown and can be served as a side dish, added to a stew, roasted on their own or in the juices of a roast. They can be braised with other vegetables such as peas, or pickled like onions. Good-quality shallots will be firm to the touch and show no signs of sprouting.

Store shallots as you would onions, in a dry location or in the refrigerator.

One of the Americas' many contributions to the rest of the world, the sweet potato was introduced to Spain in the fifteen hundreds by the early Spanish explorers, although it was already known and cultivated in Polynesia before that time. Today, this member of the morning glory family is cultivated in New Zealand, throughout the Pacific Islands, in southern Europe, China, Japan, and India, as well as in the Americas, where the swollen root continues to be a popular food.

Sweet Potato
Ipomoea batatas

Sweet potatoes are of two general categories: moist, bright-orange fleshed; and dry, light-yellow fleshed. The orange-fleshed commonly has dark reddish skin and sweeter, denser flesh than the starchier yellow-fleshed types. The former is often marketed in North America as a yam, but true yams are tropical tubers that belong to a different family and they are rarely seen in the mainland United States.

We generally think of baking or steaming sweet potatoes, but they make superb French fries, oven fries, and stir-fries, taking slightly less time to cook than Irish potatoes. Because of their substantial sugar content, sweet potatoes are used in dessert dishes—sweet potato pie immediately comes to mind—and combine well with tropical fruits such as mangoes and papayas and with coconut and citrus. In savory uses, complementary flavors are coriander, cumin, hot chilies, the Mediterraneans herbs, and hard and soft cheeses. I especially like them baked with only salt and pepper.

Most of the sweet potatoes and American yams we see in the markets are one of three main varieties: Yellow Jewel, Red Jewel, and Garnet. In Hawaii, however, the markets often stock the purple-fleshed sweet potato, which is exceedingly sweet and very beautiful, and has flesh slightly more starchy than the commonly seen mainland types. In choosing all sweet potatoes, look for firm, unshriveled specimens, free of the grayish white mold that develops on damaged or decaying roots. Store in a dry place or in the refrigerator.

Taro
Colocasia esculenta

Taro, a member of the Araceae family, grows throughout the tropical and subtropical areas of Southeast Asia, its probable origin, and has spread to Africa, the islands of the Pacific, and the West Indies. Also known as dasheen, gabi, and eddoe, it is grown from corms but produces tubers. Many, many varieties of taro exist; Hawaii alone is reputed to have had 150 different ones growing at the end of the nineteenth century.

The tubers are brown to beige, with hard ridged skin that often sports hairs. The size varies as well, from large ones weighing several pounds to "sons-of-taro," as the Chinese call the kiwi-sized tubers that grow around a single large tuber. The leaves and stems are also edible.

The flesh of larger taros tends to be crumbly when cooked, not unlike a high-starch baking potato, but the cooked flesh of the small ones is smoother and more pastelike. The taste is faintly nutty and sweet, and a hot baked taro, its skin split open like that of a baked potato and topped with butter, salt, and pepper, is delicious. Taros, both large and small, are becoming a steady item in some mainstream supermarkets, just as they have been in ethnic markets for a number of years.

Culinarily, taros may be treated like thick-skinned, starchy potatoes. They can be cooked first—either steamed or baked—mashed, and then combined with other ingredients to make, for example, savory croquettes, or eaten on their own. Or they can be added to soups and stews, or deep-fried or oven-fried to make chips. Except when baked or steamed whole, they are peeled before cooking. In traditional societies, they are most often boiled down to a sticky mass, of which Hawaiian poi is one type.

Taro is generally available year-round. A good-quality specimen will be firm, with no soft spots, feel heavy in the hand, and show no signs of mold or decay. Store taro in a dry location or in the refrigerator.

Turnips are native to both Asia and Europe, where they still grow wild. Although we most commonly see only one turnip variety in the markets of the United States—round, off-white with a purple collar—there are numerous other types. In France and Italy, one finds small, round, flat buttonlike turnips, white with bright magenta collars and usually sold quite young with leaves attached; long-rooted white ones, perhaps with a bit of pink or even green collars; and roundish cream-colored ones. In England, too, there is a wide variety of turnips, but perhaps it is in Japan and China that the greatest range exists. There are many types, sizes, and shapes of Japanese turnips, some reaching up to thirty pounds, including one favored for pickling that is long and narrow like a white carrot, but purple at the top. Of the Japanese types, my personal preference for the garden are the perfectly round, perfectly white ones that grow quickly to jawbreaker size. They are so mild that they can be eaten raw and their tender greens used in salad. Left to grow, they will become at least the size of a softball without becoming pithy, and the greens, although now they require cooking, are flavorful without being overbearingly strong, as turnip greens can be.

Like so many roots, turnips are used in diverse ways in the kitchen. They can be baked in gratins, steamed, and then puréed with cream or milk, or sliced and simmered with butter and herbs. They can be grated and used in salads or made into savory cakes, whether on their own or with grated potatoes. Stews welcome the flavor of a turnip or two, and the roots are particularly adept at absorbing pan juices from roasts. Turnips can be stir-fried, deep-fried, or oven-fried. In short, they can be used in almost every way.

Taro

Turnip

Brassica rapa, Rapifera Group

Turnip

In choosing turnips, the smaller and younger they are, the milder the flavor will be. Freshly dug turnips will usually have their green leaves attached, while the storage turnips will most likely have clipped tops. They are available year-round, although baby-sized ones are more easily found in spring and fall than in summer. Store turnips in the refrigerator.

Water Chestnut

Eleocharis dulcis

The origin of the water chestnut, a member of the Cyperaceae or Sedge family, may be found in a swath that stretches across the Old World tropics from East Asia to Madagascar and into Polynesia. Grown in flooded paddies, water chestnuts are the corms that form on the spreading rhizomes of a water-loving sedge grass, and they are dug up from the mud when the paddies are drained. Mature water chestnuts have a rather hard brown shell that must be removed in order to reach the succulent, sweet flesh beneath. Small, about the size of a tree chestnut and resembling it somewhat in outer appearance, the fresh water chestnut is as different from canned water chestnuts as ripe fresh tomatoes are from canned ones.

Water chestnuts remain firm and crunchy, even after cooking, and although the flavor is most intense when raw, they are frequently cooked. They are common ingredients in Japanese and Chinese cuisine, but are highly adaptable to Western dishes, especially salads, where they can be used raw, as you would sliced or grated carrots, for example. Complementary flavors are other crunchy roots such as jicama and carrot, sweet tropical fruits, peas, onions, and herbs such as cilantro and mint.

Another unrelated vegetable also sometimes known as a water chestnut is *Trapa bicornis,* or water caltrop, a corm that grows in the same way as the true water chestnut. It is small, black, and shiny and is easily recongized by its shape: two outward-curving horns with a tiny unicorn horn between. Starchier tasting than the Chinese water chestnut, it too must be peeled; unlike it, however, the water caltrop must be cooked before being eaten (usually boiled or steamed for an hour), as it is toxic when raw.

Fresh water chestnuts can be found most of the year, and a good specimen will be firm, without any soft spots or cracking of the shell evident. When the shell is removed, the flesh should be white; if it is yellow or otherwise discolored, discard it. Store water chestnuts in the refrigerator.

This is the true yam, a tuber belonging to the Dioscoreaceae family. Sometimes called Chinese yam, it originated in Asia and is the food staple of millions and millions of people living in tropical and subtropical regions around the world. Developing mature yam tubers takes an eight- to ten-month growing season, so yam production is not feasible in areas with temperate climates.

What is called a yam by many people in the United States is actually a type of sweet potato. The true yam looks like an irregular club with a long, narrow neck and a swelling at the end. The skin is thick, tan, and covered with sparse hairy rootlets. Sizes range from a few ounces to over one hundred pounds. Textures can go from smooth to grainy, the flavor from sweet to starchy. Large tubers grow for over a year before they are harvested and are commonly over two feet in length.

Yams can be baked, boiled, puréed, or cooked in soups and stews—in other words, used much as you would a sweet potato or Irish potato. Some yams contain toxins, however, which are destroyed only after long cooking, and thus these varieties are not suited to quick stir-frying or deep-frying. As with many other roots, look for firm specimens that show no signs of mold or decay.

Yam
Dioscorea batatas

A bland, high-starch tuber native to South America, yuca, a member of the Euphorbiaceae, has become a dietary mainstay in the tropical regions of the world. It travels under several different names—cassava, bitter casava, tapioca plant, manioc—and somewhat resembles a sweet potato in shape, but with thick, barklike skin and whitish beige flesh that is quite dry and somewhat stringy.

Yuca, like taro, makes a good chip when peeled, sliced thin, and deep-fried or oven roasted. Or it can be cut into batons and boiled until tender and then cooked as for French fries. Its dense, starchy texture lends itself to thick, puréed soups when used in conjunction with more flavorful ingredients and lively seasonings. In most parts of the world where it is grown, yuca is eaten boiled, made into flour or meal, or fermented to make a drink. The flour is used to make tapioca "beads," a popular pudding base and thickener in Europe and the United States.

Yuca
Manihot esculenta

Small Dishes

(b e e t s)

A small dish is whatever you want it to be. It might be a first course, an hors d'oeuvre for a party, a side dish, a television snack, or lunch. It might be increased in quantity to make a main course or several served together might compose the entire meal. Generally, the small root dishes presented here have relatively few other ingredients. The emphasis is on the root itself. There are suggestions made throughout, however, about how the small dish might be served or what might be a particularly good accompaniment.

a big spoonful of garlic-specked red wine vinegar is poured through a slit made in the hot wrapper. Down and over the finely minced roots and green onions it drizzles to dampen the edges of the wrapper with its pungent taste.

MAKES 12 ROLLS; SERVES 4 TO 6 AS AN APPETIZER
OR 3 AS A MAIN COURSE

3 or 4 large garlic cloves, crushed and minced

3/4 cup red wine vinegar

30 small, young or 20 medium-sized red
    radishes

8 to 10 small, young carrots

8 green onions

12 square egg roll wrappers, each about
    6 inches square

light oil such as canola for frying

Place the garlic and vinegar together in a glass bowl and set aside for several hours to allow the flavors to blend.

Remove the greens and the stringlike root tip from the radishes and carrots. Chop them both finely; you should have about 1 cup each. Set aside. Trim the green onions to approximately 6 inches long, discarding or saving for another use the upper portion of the green stalk. Cut the onions into pieces 3 inches long and then slice them lengthwise into very thin juliennelike slivers.

In the center of each egg roll wrapper, place about 1 rounded tablespoon each of the carrot and radish, and then add a few slivers of green onion. Fold the corner nearest you over the filling and then fold in the two side corners. Fold the upper corner down over all, envelope style, spreading a little water on the inner edge and pressing together to seal. As the spring rolls are filled, set them aside on waxed paper, seam side down, and cover with a damp towel to keep them moist until you are ready to cook them.

In a deep, medium-sized skillet, pour in oil to a depth of $1/2$ inch. Heat over medium-high heat until a piece of carrot or radish sizzles and bubbles when dropped into the hot oil. Reduce the heat to medium and, using tongs, place 3 or 4 of the spring rolls, seam side down, in the hot oil. They should not be touching. Fry on one side for $1^1/2$ minutes, or just until the wrapper has browned and turned crispy. Turn and cook on the other side until golden, about 1 minute. Remove the spring rolls with the tongs, holding each one over the skillet for a moment or two to allow the excess oil to drip, and set on absorbent towels or paper to drain. Repeat until all the spring rolls are cooked.

To serve, arrange on a platter or individual plates. Make an incision in the top of each roll and spoon in about 1 tablespoon of the garlic vinegar. Serve hot or at room temperature.

small dishes

Batter-Fried Salsify Fritters

SERVES 4 TO 6

4 to 5 cups cold water

3 tablespoons cider or distilled white vinegar

5 salsify or scorzonera roots, about
$^1/_2$ pound in all

$^3/_4$ cup all-purpose flour

1 cup ice water

$^1/_2$ teaspoon salt

light oil such as canola for frying

a French friend who was a young girl in Paris during World War II remembers her mother grumbling over preparing salsify, one of the few vegetables they had in abundance. Because the roots exuded a latexlike substance that stuck to her fingers, she didn't like peeling them. The family all agreed, though, that once the salsify was prepared and deep-fried in a delicate, tempura-like batter it was delicious. The dish was a mainstay of their table during and after the war years. • These crunchy fries make a tasty accompaniment to roasts, chops, salads, and soups, or a satisfying appetizer served with parsley mayonnaise for dipping. The same deep-frying technique can be used for other roots such as thinly sliced carrots, turnips, celery root, daikon radishes, and Chinese artichokes.

Put the cold water and vinegar in a nonreactive vessel. (Use a saucepan if the roots are mature, as you will need to parboil them before frying.) Using a vegetable peeler or paring knife, scrape away the skin of the salsify or scorzonera roots. Rinse them and then cut them into 2-inch lengths (about 5 pieces per root), then quarter them lengthwise to make thin sticks. Put them into the acidulated water to prevent discoloration.

If the salsify is very young and tender, it can be now be patted dry, dipped in batter, and fried. If the salsify is mature, I find it is more succulent if it is parboiled first. To parboil, bring the salsify in its vinegar water to a boil over medium heat and cook for about 8 minutes. Drain and pat dry.

Preheat an oven to 300 degrees F. In a deep skillet or heavy-bottomed saucepan, pour in oil to a depth of 2 inches and place over medium heat until hot.

While the oil is heating, put the flour and salt in a bowl and whisk or beat in the ice water (do use ice water, as it helps make the batter crisp and crunchy when fried). To test the oil for readiness, drop a bit of batter into it. Bubbles should surround it and it should start to cook immediately. Dip the salsify pieces, 4 or 5 at a time, into the batter, and then slip them into the hot oil. Fry until golden brown and cooked through, 2 to 3 minutes. Using a slotted spoon or tongs, remove the fritters to absorbent towels or paper to drain. Place in the oven until all the fritters have been fried. Serve hot.

New Potato, Celery Root, and Portobello Mushroom Turnovers

although making these turnovers might look like a lengthy process, it actually takes little more than half an hour from start to the delivery of a batch of flaky show-off turnovers to the table. Other versions might be made using young turnips, rutabagas, or taro instead of the potatoes.

MAKES 4 TURNOVERS; SERVES 4

Preheat an oven to 425 degrees F.

Cut the potatoes, peeled or unpeeled as you prefer, into $1/2$-inch cubes. With a paring knife, peel the celery root, then cut it into pieces of the same size. You should have about 2 cups diced potatoes and about $1^1/2$ cups diced celery root. Put them together in a bowl and add the thyme, sage, $1/2$ teaspoon of the salt, $1/2$ teaspoon of the pepper, and 2 to 3 tablespoons of the olive oil. Turn to coat well. Spread the mixture in a single layer on a baking sheet and place in the oven. Cook for 6 or 7 minutes, then, using a spatula, turn the cubes. Cook for another 7 or 8 minutes, or until the vegetables are tender and have formed a slightly golden crust.

While the vegetables are cooking, make the turnover dough. In a bowl, sift together the flour and 1 teaspoon of the salt. Cut the $1/2$ cup butter into 1-inch pieces and add to the bowl. Using a pastry blender or 2 knives, cut the butter into the flour until they have blended to make large pea-sized pieces. Add the ice water and finish blending the mixture with your fingertips, working the dough just enough to be able to combine the whole into a ball. Wrap with waxed paper or plastic wrap and refrigerate until needed.

Remove the vegetables from the oven and set aside. Leave the oven set at 425 degrees F.

Cut the mushroom vertically into $1/4$-inch-thick slices, including the stem. Add the remaining 1 tablespoon butter and 1 tablespoon olive oil to a small skillet and place over medium heat until the butter melts and begins to foam. Add the garlic and sauté a minute or two, then add the mushroom slices. Cook for 3 or 4 minutes, turning occasionally. The slices will begin to release their juices. Add the parsley and the remaining $1/4$ teaspoon salt and $1/2$ teaspoon pepper, and continue cooking until the slices are soft and have changed color, another minute or two. Remove from the heat. Cut the mushroom slices into small pieces; reserve the mushroom juice.

5 or 6 small waxy potatoes such as Yellow Finn
  or Yukon Gold, about $1^1/2$ pounds in all

1 small celery root, about $1/2$ pound

1 tablespoon minced fresh thyme

1 tablespoon minced fresh sage

1 $3/4$ teaspoons salt

1 teaspoon freshly ground black pepper

3 to 4 tablespoons olive oil

2 cups all-purpose flour

$1/2$ cup plus 1 tablespoon unsalted butter

6 tablespoons ice water

1 large, fresh portobello mushroom,
  brushed clean

1 garlic clove, minced

2 tablespoons minced fresh parsley

1 egg yolk mixed with 1 tablespoon water

Divide the dough into 4 equal portions. On a lightly floured work surface, roll out each portion into a round 8 inches in diameter and $1/4$ inch thick. Place an equal amount of the potato–celery root mixture on the center of one-half of each round. Spoon the mushroom pieces and their juices atop the potato–celery root mounds, again dividing equally. Fold over each round to make a half-moon, spreading a little water on the inner edges and pressing together to seal. Brush the tops with the egg yolk mixture, and then pierce the tops with the tines of a fork to allow steam to vent.

Put the turnovers on an ungreased baking sheet. Bake until the tops are golden, 13 to 15 minutes. Serve hot.

Red Radish Cream Tea Sandwiches

finely minced bits of red radish give a crunchy texture and a slightly different note to this addition to the usual English teatime selection of sandwiches. For bread, consider a dark rye or a home-style white bread.

MAKES 3 OR 4 SANDWICHES

1 cup minced red radishes (about 20)

1 teaspoon poppyseeds

1 cup mascarpone cheese

6 or 8 slices rye bread

$3/4$ teaspoon salt

24 young arugula or lettuce leaves

In a bowl, combine the radishes, poppyseeds, mascarpone, and salt, mixing until well blended. Let stand for 10 minutes to allow the flavors to blend.

Cover half of the bread slices with a generous $1/4$-inch-thick layer of the mascarpone mixture, top with 6 or 8 arugula or lettuce leaves, and cover with another slice of bread. Cut the sandwiches in triangular halves for an English look and serve.

Buttered Dill Beets

3 large beets, any kind, about 1¹/₄ pounds
     in all

3 tablespoons butter

¹/₄ to ¹/₂ teaspoon salt

¹/₂ teaspoon freshly ground black pepper

3 tablespoons minced fresh dill

For many root vegetables, a little butter and a well-chosen fresh herb are all that is needed to bring out their unique character. Beets and dill seem made for each other, but tarragon, chervil, and chives are also flavor elevators for them and for carrots. For Chinese artichokes, a sprinkling of parsley or chervil is a suitable partner, but the more strongly flavored rutabagas, turnips, and onions can be paired with the woody Mediterranean herbs of thyme and rosemary as well as the green herbs.

Cut off all but 1 inch of the beet tops and save for another use. Place the beets in a large saucepan with enough water to cover them by 2 or 3 inches. Bring to a boil, cover the pan, reduce the heat to low, and simmer until tender when pierced with the tip of a sharp knife and the skins will slip off easily, 1 to 1¹/₂ hours; the timing will depend upon the size and maturity of the beets. Alternatively, place the trimmed beets on a steamer rack over boiling water, cover, and steam until tender, about 1¹/₄ hours.

Drain well (or remove from the steamer rack) and let stand until they are cool enough to handle, then slip off the skins with your fingers or use a paring knife. Cut the beets into the desired size and shape—bite-sized cubes, wedges, or slices—and put them in a saucepan with the butter, salt, and pepper. Place over low heat and turn the beets as the butter melts. Continue turning the beets until they are hot all the way through, then stir in the dill and serve.

Plates of dim sum, small, mostly savory dishes, are traditionally eaten from mid-morning to early afternoon with tea in southern China and in Chinese communities around the world. In restaurants, rolling carts laden with an array of different dishes are pushed among the tables in a seemingly endless flow. At tableside, lids are lifted from steaming baskets and tiny plates to reveal perhaps two or three pork buns, a mound of slippery noodles, hot pot stickers, or shrimp or pork rolls, and people choose the dishes they want. • Water chestnuts figure in many of the dim sum fillings. Here, bite-sized squares of green pepper are topped with a mild and savory blend and steamed, but the same mixture could be used to fill pot stickers or other dumplings.

With a paring knife, peel away the hard, dark shell-like skin of the water chestnuts. Finely chop the creamy white meat. You should have about $3/4$ cup. Place in a bowl and add the pork, shrimp, ginger, $1^{1}/2$ tablespoons soy sauce, cilantro, and egg white. Mix well.

Cut off the stem of each bell pepper and discard. Cut the peppers in half lengthwise and remove and discard the seeds and any inner core. Cut the halves into $1^{1}/2$-inch squares. On the inside surface of each square, mound about 2 tablespoons of the filling. Place the squares on a steamer rack and place the rack in a pan over boiling water. Cover and steam until the peppers are tender and the filling is cooked, 8 to 10 minutes.

Remove to a platter or individual plates and serve hot with soy sauce or a mixture of soy sauce and sesame oil.

MAKES ABOUT 18 SQUARES;
SERVES 6 AS AN APPETIZER

15 fresh water chestnuts

$1/2$ pound ground pork

$1/4$ pound cooked baby shrimp

2 tablespoons grated fresh ginger

1 $1/2$ tablespoons soy sauce

2 tablespoons minced fresh cilantro

1 egg white

2 to 3 green bell peppers

soy sauce or mixture of soy sauce and Asian
   sesame oil for serving

small dishes

Sweet Potato Gnocchi

MAKES ABOUT 100 GNOCCHI; SERVES 4 TO 6

Similar in shape to Italian potato gnocchi, these pale golden dumplings have a smoother texture and the characteristic taste of sweet potatoes. Served with a roast and topped with its juices, they make a fine accompaniment, or offer them on their own, crowned with a little butter, grated Parmesan cheese, and then gratinéed, as here. Orange-fleshed sweet potatoes are not suitable for this recipe; choose instead the starchy, yellow-fleshed ones.

1 1/2 pounds yellow-fleshed sweet potatoes

1 pound Russet or other similar high-starch
   Irish baking potato

1 egg

1 cup all-purpose flour, plus flour for dusting

2 teaspoons salt

1/4 cup minced fresh parsley

1 1/2 tablespoons butter, cut into small pieces

1 tablespoon freshly ground black pepper

2 tablespoons freshly grated Parmesan
   cheese

Preheat an oven to 350 degrees F.

Place all the potatoes on a baking sheet. Bake until they are soft all the way to the center when pierced with the tines of a fork, about 1 hour for medium-sized Russets and 50 minutes for medium-sized sweet potatoes. Remove from the oven and let cool until they can be easily handled, about 15 minutes.

Peel the skins from the Russets, then, using the large holes of a hand-held grater, grate them into a large bowl. Peel the sweet potatoes and grate them into the bowl. Add the egg and, using an electric mixer set on medium speed, beat until fluffy, about 1 minute. Add the 1 cup flour, 1/2 teaspoon of the salt, and the parsley, and beat again just long enough to incorporate all the ingredients.

Fill a large pot three-quarters full with water and bring to a boil over high heat. While the water is heating, make the gnocchi: Lightly flour a work surface and turn the potato mixture onto it. Take a large handful of the dough and roll it first between the palms of your hands to make a rope about 8 inches long. Then, using your palms, roll it on the work surface into a rope 12 inches long and 1 inch in diameter. Cut the rope in half. Roll half of the rope in the same manner to form another 12-inch-long rope, this one about 1/2 inch in diameter. Repeat with the other half of the original rope. Cut each rope into 1/2-inch-long pieces. Lightly dust the pieces with flour and set them aside on a tray or platter. Cover them with a damp cloth until you are ready to cook them. Repeat this process, washing the stickiness from your hands as necessary, until all of the dough has been formed into gnocchi.

Preheat an oven to 250 degrees F. Place an ovenproof serving dish large enough to hold all the cooked gnocchi in the oven.

When the water is boiling and just before adding the gnocchi, add 1 teaspoon of the salt to the pot. Using a slotted spoon, slip the gnocchi into the boiling water 2 or 3 dozen at a time: do not crowd them in the pot. (You can cook the gnocchi all at once by using 2 large pots of water.) Cook the gnocchi 2 or 3 minutes, jogging them gently with a wooden spoon after a minute or two. They are done as soon as they float to the surface; cut into one to be sure. Remove them with a slotted spoon to the warmed dish and return it to the oven. Cook the remaining gnocchi in the same way.

When all the gnocchi are cooked, top them evenly with the butter, the remaining $1/2$ teaspoon salt, the pepper, and cheese. Increase the oven heat to 400 degrees F and return the serving dish to the oven. Cook the gnocchi for 8 to 10 minutes, or until the butter has melted. Serve piping hot.

Fresh Horseradish Sauce

a spoonful of fresh horseradish sauce atop a raw oyster or alongside slices of juicy prime rib or corned beef heightens their flavors and allows horseradish lovers to indulge themselves. Although some people like to use pure grated horseradish, I find that adding a little cream, mayonnaise, and mustard smooths out both the texture and taste of the root. This recipe yields two cups, but any amount can be made by simply adjusting the quantities. I recommend making just what you are going to use immediately, as the horseradish rapidly loses its potency once it is grated.

MAKES ABOUT 2 CUPS

Using a paring knife, peel the tough outer skin off the root, protecting your hands with rubber gloves, if necessary, and being careful not to rub your eyes. Grate the root on a hand-held grater into a bowl. The fine holes of the grater produce a fine, fluffy texture; the larger holes create a coarse, shredded result. I like both.

Stir in the cream and the mayonnaise and mustard, if desired. If you do have leftover sauce, put it in a glass jar with a tight-fitting cover and store it in the refrigerator, where it will keep for up to 1 week.

1 horseradish root, about $3/4$ pound

$1/4$ cup heavy cream

4 to 6 tablespoons homemade or prepared
   mayonnaise (optional)

1 tablespoon Dijon mustard (optional)

Spicy Sweet Potato Wontons

MAKES 16 TO 20; SERVES 4 AS AN APPETIZER

The dense, soft texture of the sweet potato sharpened with ginger and chili juxtaposes harmoniously with the crisp flakiness of the wonton wrapper to make an unusual appetizer. If you want to serve the wontons with something extra, mix a favorite chutney with lime juice for a dipping sauce, or serve them alongside a salad of mixed baby Asian greens or of young, nutty arugula tossed with small pieces of perfectly ripe melon or orange.

2 yellow- or orange-fleshed sweet potatoes, about 1/2 pound each

3 tablespoons minced fresh ginger

1/2 cup chopped fresh cilantro

3 fresh serrano chilies, seeded and minced

1/4 teaspoon salt

16 to 20 round wonton wrappers, each 3 1/2 inches in diameter

light oil such as canola for frying

Preheat an oven to 375 degrees F.

Place the sweet potatoes in a baking dish. Bake them until they are soft all the way to the center when pierced with the tines of a fork, about 1 hour.

Remove the sweet potatoes from the oven and let cool until they can be easily handled, about 15 minutes. Cut them in half and, with a large spoon, scrape the soft pulp from the skin into a bowl, omitting any of the pulp that has been discolored during baking. You will have about 1 cup. Add the ginger, cilantro, chilies, and salt and mix well.

To fill each round wonton, place 1 tablespoon of the sweet potato mixture in the middle of a wrapper. Fold the wrapper over to make a half-moon, spreading a little water on the inner edges and pressing together to seal. As the wontons are filled, set them aside on waxed paper and cover with a damp towel to keep them moist until you are ready to cook them.

In a wok or deep skillet, pour in oil to a depth of 1/2 inch. Heat the oil over medium-high heat until it sizzles when a drop of water hits it. Reduce the heat to medium and, using tongs, place the wontons, a few at a time, into the hot oil. Fry on one side until the wonton skins are golden and slightly puffed, about 1 minute. Turn and fry on the other side until golden, 30 or 40 seconds. Remove the wontons with the tongs, holding each one over the pan for a moment or two to allow any excess oil to drip, and set on absorbent towels or paper to drain. Repeat until all the wontons are cooked. Serve hot.

Some dishes—cracked crab, crayfish—are meant to be eaten in company, with much licking of fingers. This is one of them. Their exterior skin roasted to deep brown, the meat of the cloves nearly caramelized and bubbling just a bit across the cut top, the whole heads of garlic come to the table ready for nimble fingers to pluck them apart. • Roasted garlic is sweet and mild and matches perfectly with slightly sour fresh cheeses such as goat cheeses. Black bread, the old-fashioned kind made with molasses, goes especially well, but so does a good French baguette.

SERVES 4

Preheat an oven to 300 degrees F.

Using a sharp knife, cut off the top $1/2$ to $3/4$ inch of the whole garlic heads. Do not remove the papery skin. Rub each head with 1 tablespoon of the olive oil, $1/2$ teaspoon of the salt, $1/2$ teaspoon of the pepper, and 1 tablespoon of the thyme. Place the heads upright in a shallow baking dish just large enough to hold them. Dot each head with $1/2$ tablespoon of the butter.

Roast, uncovered, for 20 minutes. Cover loosely with aluminum foil and bake until the cloves are soft and easily pierced with the tip of a sharp knife, about 20 minutes longer. Remove and let cool until they can be handled easily, about 15 minutes.

To serve, place a whole head of roasted garlic, a portion of cheese, and a slice of the bread on each of 4 plates. Place the remaining cheese and bread on the table. To eat the garlic, peel away the crispy outer layer of skin from the heads and discard it. Separate the cloves and, squeezing from the bottom, "pop" the soft, aromatic meat from the thin, papery covering. Spread the garlic on the bread with a little cheese.

4 medium-sized heads firm, fresh garlic

4 tablespoons olive oil

2 teaspoons salt

2 teaspoons freshly ground black pepper

4 tablespoons minced fresh thyme

2 tablespoons butter, cut into bits

$1/2$ pound fresh goat cheese or other
   similar cheese

1 loaf black, rye, pumpernickel, or other
   bread, sliced

small dishes

Prosciutto-Wrapped Salsify

SERVES 4 TO 5

The delicate oysterlike taste of salsify, perked with a little tarragon mayonnaise, finds a fit companion in a wrapping of thinly sliced prosciutto or other fine cured ham.

4 cups water

3 tablespoons cider or distilled white vinegar

4 salsify or scorzonera roots, about 1/2 pound
   in all

6 tablespoons homemade or prepared
   mayonnaise

2 tablespoons white wine vinegar

6 tablespoons minced fresh tarragon, plus
   tarragon sprigs for garnish

1/4 pound thinly sliced prosciutto or cooked ham

Put the water and the cider or distilled white vinegar in a nonreactive saucepan and set aside. Using a vegetable peeler or paring knife, scrape away the skin of the salsify or scorzonera roots. Rinse and then cut them into 2-inch lengths (about 5 pieces per root) and put them into the acidulated water to prevent discoloration. (If you prefer longer lengths, adjust the size of the prosciutto or ham wrappers accordingly.)

When all the roots are peeled and cut, place the saucepan over high heat and bring to a boil. Reduce the heat to medium-high and boil for about 10 minutes. (If the roots are small and young, 5 to 6 minutes will be adequate.) The roots are done when they can be easily pierced with the tip of a sharp knife. They should be firm but tender, not soft and mushy. Remove the pan from the heat and drain, then rinse with cold water. Pat dry and set aside.

In a small bowl, combine the mayonnaise, white wine vinegar, and tarragon and mix well. Cut the prosciutto or ham into pieces approximately 2 inches by 3 inches, or large enough to wrap the root lengths fully. Wrap each root length with a piece of prosciutto and set aside.

To serve, divide the wrapped roots among 4 or 5 small plates. Place a generous tablespoonful of the tarragon mayonnaise alongside and garnish each plate with a sprig of tarragon. Or arrange the wrapped roots on a platter, garnish the platter with tarragon sprigs, and place the mayonnaise in a bowl alongside.

a number of roots mash well with potatoes to create a variation on a favorite theme. Potatoes can be cooked and puréed with many other roots, including parsnips, turnips, rutabagas, carrots, celery root, and parsley root. The end flavor of the dish depends upon the proportions used. A little rutabaga goes a long way, but even a hint of it gives a robust taste to the potatoes. Here, the pungent earthiness of parsley root is an equal partner with the potato.

SERVES 4 TO 6

Cut the potatoes, peeled or unpeeled as you prefer, into 4 or 5 pieces. With a vegetable peeler or a paring knife, scrape off the hairy rootlets and buff skin of the parsley roots and cut them into 1-inch pieces. Put the potatoes and parsley root pieces in a saucepan and add water to cover generously. Add 1 teaspoon of the salt and bring the water to a boil over medium-high heat. Reduce the heat to medium-low, cover partially, and cook until the potatoes are easily pierced with the tines of a fork, about 15 minutes.

Drain the potatoes and parsley roots and return them to the saucepan to mash them. Mashing them in the pan helps them to stay hot. Combine the milk and half-and-half in a measuring pitcher and add about 1/4 cup of the mixture to the pan. Using a hand masher or an electric mixer, mash the potatoes and parsley roots, adding as much of the remaining milk mixture as needed, a little at a time, until they reach the consistency you want. Stir in the butter, the remaining 1 teaspoon salt, and the pepper.

Transfer to a serving dish and garnish with the minced parsley. Serve hot.

6 medium-sized potatoes, preferably a boiling type such as White Rose, Red Rose or Yukon Gold, about 2 1/2 pounds in all

4 to 6 parsley roots, about 1/4 pound in all

2 teaspoons salt

1/2 cup milk

1/2 cup half-and-half

2 tablespoons butter

1 teaspoon freshly ground black pepper

1/2 cup minced fresh parsley

Scalloped Potatoes Layered with Anchovies

SERVES 4

anchovies and rosemary combine to perfume a dish of humble potatoes. As the casserole slowly bakes, the potatoes absorb the sauce to become imbued with a taste of the Mediterranean. This makes an excellent accompaniment for roasts of all kinds and for game birds with character.

1 tablespoon butter

6 medium-sized potatoes, either baking type
   such as russet ot waxy type such as
   Yukon Gold, about 2^1/$_2$ pounds in all

2 large white or yellow onions

6 anchovy fillets packed in olive oil, cut into
   ^{1}/$_2$-inch pieces

1 tablespoon chopped fresh rosemary

1^1/$_2$ cups heavy cream

oil from the anchovy tin

1 teaspoon freshly ground black pepper

Peel the potatoes and cut them lengthwise, French-fry style, into batons ^{1}/$_2$ inch thick. Set aside. Slice the onions into rounds about ^{1}/$_4$ inch thick and set these aside also.

Preheat an oven to 350 degrees F. Butter a 2-quart baking dish, preferably one with a fitted lid. Arrange about one-third of the potatoes in a layer in the prepared dish. Scatter about half of the anchovy pieces over them and sprinkle with about half of the rosemary. Top with a layer of half the onions. Repeat using half of the remaining potatoes and all of the remaining anchovies, rosemary, and onion. Layer the remaining potatoes on top.

In a pitcher, stir together ^{3}/$_4$ cup of the cream and all of the oil from the anchovy tin. Pour the mixture over the top of the potatoes. Cover the dish with its lid, or cover and seal with aluminum foil.

Place it in the oven and bake for 35 minutes. Remove from the oven, remove the lid or cover, and pour the remaining cream evenly over the potatoes. Sprinkle the top with the pepper. Cover again and bake until the potatoes are tender enough to break apart when pierced with the tines of a fork, about 15 minutes longer. Serve hot, spooned from the baking dish.

Grilled Leeks and Green Garlic

24 baby leeks or heads of green garlic

1/3 cup olive oil

1/2 teaspoon salt

1 teaspoon freshly ground black pepper

3 tablespoons chopped fresh marjoram
   or thyme

Two of the finest of the *Allium* genus's contributions to the table are young leeks and garlic, which are delicious slightly charred on a grill or under a broiler after having been rubbed with olive oil and seasonings. They can be served on platters as you would French fries or onion rings, laid alongside a juicy steak or chop, or chopped for topping breads or other vegetables such as baked potatoes, simmered herbed tomatoes, or fresh corn.

Trim the leeks or green garlic, removing approximately one-third of the green tops. Wash well. If the root end of the stalk is larger than 1/2 inch in diameter, slit it lengthwise but leave it intact. Lay the stalks in a shallow glass or ceramic dish and drizzle them with the olive oil, then sprinkle on the salt, pepper, and marjoram. Turn the stalks in the oil and marinate at room temperature for at least 1 hour or up to 6 hours.

Build a charcoal fire in a grill, or preheat a broiler.

When the fire is ready or the broiler is hot, remove the leeks or garlic from the marinade and arrange them on an oiled grill rack or a broiler pan. Grill or broil, turning as needed, until tender and faintly charred, 2 to 3 minutes on each side.

Serve hot or at room temperature.

leeks

Salads

jicama

Roots, raw or cooked, are eminently suited to salad making of all genres. This is true in large part because so many of them can be eaten raw, an aspect important to health, convenience, and flavor. A simple presentation of young radishes with a leaf or two yet attached, served with a little salt, country bread, and butter, is one of the best salads I know. Raw carrots and celery or parsley roots can be treated to a sprinkle of lemon juice, a vinaigrette, or a seasoned mayonnaise. Building on this base, you can add chicken, smoked fish, fruits, nuts, watercress or other greens, or cheeses to make more complex salads, mixed or composed. The less familiar jicama, Jerusalem artichokes, and fresh water chestnuts can be used raw in salads, too, where they are complemented by lime and orange juice, by the bite of chilies and the sweetness of fruits.

Once cooked, potatoes and beets are natural salad ingredients. Indeed, potato salad is one of the great dishes of all time, and renditions of it are as varied as the people preparing them. Parboiled first, Chinese artichokes and lotus roots, although certainly not as well-known in the United States as beets and potatoes, make interesting salad ingredients to combine with greens, onions, carrots—in short, with almost anything.

Crunchy Tortilla Salad

SERVES 4

In this colorful construction, *crema* (Mexican sour cream), seasoned with freshly ground dried chili added just before serving, blends together the wild flavors of jicama and watercress, of green chili and chicken. Piled high on a bed of radishes, green onions, red lettuce, and crumbled tortilla chips, this light salad makes a main dish meal.

1 to 2 dried pasilla chilies

1 1/3 cups *crema,* or 1 cup regular or light sour cream thinned with 1/3 cup half-and-half

1/2 teaspoon salt

4 lemons

1 small to medium-sized jicama, about 1/2 pound

2 cups shredded cooked chicken (from about 2 whole breasts)

1 cup watercress leaves, plus several watercress sprigs for garnish

2 fresh green Anaheim or other mild green chilies, seeded and minced

2 cups torn red or green lettuce leaves (bite-sized pieces)

1/2 cup minced red radishes, plus 8 red radishes, trimmed, for garnish

1/2 cup minced green onions, including tender greens, plus 4 green onions, trimmed, for garnish

4 cups tortilla chips, crushed

Remove the seeds and stems from the dried chilies. Cut the chilies coarsely and then, using a spice grinder, small electric coffee mill, or a blender, grind them into a coarse powder. Measure out 1/4 cup of the powder and reserve the remainder for another use. In a small bowl, combine the *crema*, the 1/4 cup chili powder, and the salt. Squeeze the juice from 2 of the lemons (about 1/4 cup) and add to the bowl. Stir to mix well. Pour half of the *crema* mixture into a small bowl and set aside.

With a paring knife, peel the jicama and then cut it into 1/4-inch dice. You should have about 1 cup. Place it in another bowl and add the chicken, watercress leaves, and minced green chili. Pour the remaining half of the *crema* mixture over all and turn the ingredients until they are well coated. Set aside.

Divide the lettuce, minced radishes, and minced green onions evenly among 4 salad plates or bowls. Squeeze the juice from the remaining 2 lemons (about 1/4 cup) and dress each serving with an equal amount of the juice, about 1 tablespoon per serving. Top each serving with an equal amount of the crushed chips, and then with the chicken mixture, dividing it equally as well. Garnish with the whole radishes, green onions, and watercress sprigs. Serve the remaining *crema* mixture on the side.

jicama and sweet winter pears are similar in their firm, crunchy texture, but dissimilar in taste. Brought together with a dressing of lime juice and chili and a crumbling of feta, the root vegetable and the fruit form a pleasing partnership. Serve as a first course or as a side salad and, if you like, use Belgian endive in place of the watercress.

With a paring knife, peel the jicama. Cut it into $^1/_4$-inch cubes and measure out 1 cup. Set aside. Reserve any leftovers for another use. Peel, halve, and core the pears, then cut them lengthwise into very thin slices.

In a small bowl, combine the lime juice, chili powder, salt, and ginger and stir well to make the dressing.

Divide the watercress leaves evenly among 4 salad plates. Arrange a thinly sliced pear half on each plate, and sprinkle each with an equal portion of the diced jicama. Drizzle the dressing over the salads and then strew the cheese evenly over the tops.

SERVES 4

1 small to medium-sized jicama, about
$^1/_2$ pound

2 winter pears such as Bosc, Red Bartlett,
or Nellis

$^1/_3$ cup fresh lime juice (from 5 or 6 limes)

1 teaspoon ground dried Anaheim or pasilla
chili, preferably freshly ground

$^1/_2$ teaspoon salt

1 teaspoon grated fresh ginger

2 cups watercress leaves

2 ounces feta, pecorino, or other similar
cheese, crumbled

Jicama and Melon Salad

SERVES 4 TO 6

jicama and melon are common companions in Mexican salads, where they are dressed up with hot chilies and cool tropical fruits and dashed with lime. Sometimes the fruits and jicama are bite-sized, and other times chopped very fine to create a salsa-like salad. In either case, jicama, because it so readily absorbs the sweet juices and hot chili taste, handily dispenses with its characteristic blandness.

1 jicama, about 3/4 pound

2 cups peeled, seeded, and diced mixed
  melons such as cantaloupe, orange- or
  green-fleshed honeydew, casaba, or
  other melons, in any combination

1/2 very ripe papaya, peeled, seeded, and diced

1 tablespoon minced fresh green chili such
  as serrano or jalapeño

1/4 cup fresh lime juice (from 3 or 4 limes)

1/4 cup crumbled feta cheese (1 ounce)

1/4 cup minced fresh cilantro

1 teaspoon ground ancho or other ground
  dried chili

With a paring knife, peel the jicama and then dice it. You should have about 1 1/2 cups. Combine the jicama, melons, papaya, and fresh chili in a bowl. Add the lime juice and turn to coat the jicama and fruits with the juice. Top with the feta, cilantro, and ground chili.

Serve immediately, or let stand before serving. Note, however, that the longer the mixture stands before serving, the more potent it will become.

Daikon Radish Salad with Rice Vinegar and Thai Basil

This peppery salad is a good choice to serve with stir-fry dishes, sushi, or grilled fish. It can also be tucked into wrappers, such as spring roll skins or lettuce leaves, along with bits of pork, beef, or vegetables. If you cannot find fresh Thai basil at your market, substitute larger-leaved Italian basil, purple basil, or cilantro.

SERVES 4

With a vegetable peeler or paring knife, peel the daikon radish. On the large holes of a hand-held grater, grate enough of the daikon radish to measure 3 cups. Reserve any remaining radish for another use. Using your hand, squeeze the liquid from the grated radish. Once squeezed, you will have approximately 2 cups. Set aside.

In a small bowl, combine the fish sauce, chili paste, and rice vinegar. Stir to mix well. Place the grated radish in a bowl, add the vinegar mixture, and toss well. Add the basil and toss to mix again.

To serve, pile the radish mixture into a peak on a flat serving dish and garnish with the basil sprig.

1 medium-sized white daikon radish, about 3/4 pound

1 teaspoon fish sauce

1 teaspoon Chinese chili paste

1/4 cup sweet rice vinegar

3 tablespoons julienned fresh Thai basil leaves,
   plus 1 basil sprig for garnish

Double Celery Turkey Salad

SERVES 3 OR 4

The mixture of celery root and celery stalks gives this salad its refreshing taste. Although chicken can be used, turkey's flavorful dark meat both sets off and enhances the pungency of the double celery. Parsley root and leaf parsley can play the same role. The salad can be either a main dish presented on a bed of greens or a side salad, plus it makes a stand-out sandwich filling.

With a paring knife, peel the skin from the celery root. Grate it on the large holes of a handheld grater to measure about 1 cup. Mince the celery stalks.

Put the two celeries into a bowl and add all the remaining ingredients. Stir to mix well and serve.

1 small to medium-sized celery root, about 3/4 pound

4 celery stalks

2 cups diced cooked turkey or chicken, chilled

2 tablespoons light sour cream

2 tablespoons homemade or prepared mayonnaise

1 teaspoon Dijon mustard

1 1/2 tablespoons Champagne or white wine vinegar

1/2 teaspoon salt

1/2 teaspoon freshly ground black pepper

1/4 cup pine nuts

1/4 cup dried pitted cherries, halved

salads

Warm Beet and Toasted Pecan Salad with Chervil-Orange Vinaigrette

SERVES 4

6 small beets, one kind or a mixture

3/4 cup pecan halves

1 lemon

3/4 cup fresh orange juice (from about 4
   oranges)

1/4 teaspoon salt

1 teaspoon freshly ground black pepper

2 teaspoons olive oil

1 1/4 cups fresh chervil leaves

1/2 cup watercress leaves

beets and oranges are natural complements. In a warm combination, the flavors of both are distinctive, here highlighted by the richness of the pecans.

Cut off all but 1 inch from the beet tops and save for another use. Place the beets in a saucepan with enough water to cover by 2 or 3 inches. If the beets are different colors, cook them separately. Bring to a boil, cover, reduce the heat to low, and simmer until tender when pierced with the tip of a sharp knife and the skins slip off easily, about 40 minutes.

Alternatively, place the trimmed beets on a steamer rack over boiling water, cover, and steam until tender, about 1 1/2 hours. Drain well (or remove from the steamer rack) and let stand until cool enough to handle, then slip off the skins with your finger or use a paring knife. Cut the beets into 1/4-inch-thick rounds. Set aside in a bowl, covering the bowl to keep them warm.

While the beets are cooking, place the pecans in a single layer in a nonstick skillet over low heat. Toast attentively for about 5 minutes, turning often to make sure the oil-rich pecans do not burn. When done, set aside to cool. Chop each half into several pieces, reserving 12 intact halves for garnishing.

To make the vinaigrette, remove the zest from the lemon, then cut it into thin julienne strips to measure 1 tablespoon. Place in a small bowl and squeeze 1 teaspoon of the juice from the lemon into the bowl as well. Add the orange juice, salt, pepper, and olive oil and whisk to dissolve the salt. Take 1/4 cup of the chervil leaves and mince them to measure about 3 tablespoons. Add these to the orange juice mixture, stirring well.

Divide the remaining chervil leaves and the watercress leaves evenly among 4 salad plates, or arrange them on a single serving platter. Top with the warm beets and pour the vinaigrette evenly over them. Strew the pecan pieces over the beets and garnish with the reserved pecan halves. Serve immediately.

The juice from the pickled herrings is used to make the dressing, which in turn gives the beets a slightly pickled taste. Tart apples add crunch as well as absorbing a hint of the pickling flavor themselves, and they, like the onions, become a lovely pink, colored by the beets. Ideally, prepare this dish a day before you plan to serve it to allow the flavors to blend fully. Serve as a first course or as part of a buffet supper.

SERVES 6 TO 8

Cut off all but 1 inch from the beet tops and save for another use. Place the beets in a saucepan with enough water to cover them by 2 or 3 inches. Bring to a boil, cover, reduce the heat to low, and simmer until tender when pierced with the tip of a sharp knife and the skins slip off easily, 1 to 1 1/2 hours; the timing will depend upon the size and maturity of the beets.

Alternatively, place the trimmed beets on a steamer rack over boiling water, cover, and steam until tender, about 1 1/2 hours. Drain well (or remove from the steamer rack) and let stand until they are cool enough to handle, then slip off the skins with your fingers or use a paring knife. Cut the beets into 1/4-inch-thick rounds and place in a large bowl.

Meanwhile, place the onion slices in a saucepan and add the water, vinegar, sugar, and salt. Bring to a boil over medium-high heat, cover, reduce the heat to low, and simmer until the onions are very tender, about 45 minutes. Remove the saucepan from the heat and pour the contents into a bowl to cool.

While the onions are cooling, prepare the apples. They may be peeled or unpeeled, as you like. Core them and cut them into bite-sized pieces. Add the apples and the cooled onions and their liquid to the bowl holding the beets.

Remove the herring fillets from their pickling brine, reserving the brine. Cut them into bite-sized pieces and add them to the bowl as well. Gently toss all the ingredients together. Strain the reserved herring liquid and add to taste to the beet mixture. Cover and refrigerate overnight to allow the flavors to blend fully. Serve chilled.

3 large red beets, about 1 1/4 pounds in all

1/2 yellow onion, cut into 1/4-inch-thick slices

3/4 cup water

1/4 cup white wine vinegar

1 tablespoon sugar

1/2 teaspoon salt

2 firm, tart green apples such as Granny Smith

1 jar (8 ounces) pickled herring fillets

Jerusalem Artichoke and Pea Shoot Salad

SERVES 4

Thin slices of nutty Jerusalem artichokes and sprightly pea shoots are piled high to make a light and airy salad dressed with a mint-and-lemon vinaigrette. Fresh water chestnuts can be substituted for the Jerusalem artichokes, as can jicama. Be sure to use pea shoots from edible-pea plants *(Pisum sativum)* and not from sweet-pea flowers, as the latter are poisonous. This is a particularly nice salad to accompany seafood such as poached salmon or pan-seared scallops or prawns.

2 large or 3 or 4 small Jerusalem
    artichokes, about 1 pound in all
1/2 cup chopped fresh mint, plus 12 mint leaves
1/3 cup Champagne vinegar or rice wine
    vinegar
1/2 teaspoon sugar
1/4 cup light oil such as canola
1/2 teaspoon salt
1/2 teaspoon freshly ground black pepper
1 cup young, tender pea shoots

With a vegetable peeler or paring knife, peel the Jerusalem artichokes. Quarter them lengthwise, then cut the quarters into very thin slices. Set aside. In a bowl, combine the chopped mint, vinegar, sugar, oil, salt, and pepper, whisking or stirring them together to create a vinaigrette. Add the sliced Jerusalem artichokes to the vinaigrette and turn them gently to coat well.

Arrange the pea shoots on 4 salad plates, dividing them evenly. Using a slotted spoon, remove the slices from the vinaigrette and place them atop the pea shoots. Drizzle the vinaigrette over each plate, garnish with the mint leaves, and serve.

Lotus Root Salad

SERVES 4

2 lotus roots, about 1 1/2 pounds in all

1 teaspoon salt

2 tablespoons soy sauce

2 tablespoons Asian sesame oil

1 tablespoon rice wine vinegar

1 teaspoon grated fresh ginger

1/2 teaspoon sugar

2 cups mixed baby Asian greens such as mizuna,
    red mustard, and tat-soi, in any combination
    or baby spinach or mixed baby lettuces

Lotus root retains its crisp texture after blanching, and its bland taste takes well to the spicy dressing here. The same dressing and presentation could be used with water chestnuts or Chinese artichokes.

With a paring knife, peel the lotus roots. Cut them into 1/4-inch-thick slices to measure 3 cups. Reserve any remaining lotus root for another use. Place the slices in a saucepan, add water to cover and the salt, and bring to a boil. Boil, uncovered, for 10 minutes. They should be crunchy yet tender. Remove from the heat, drain, and plunge the slices into a bowl of cold water to stop the cooking. Drain again and set aside.

In a small bowl, combine the soy sauce, sesame oil, vinegar, ginger, and sugar and whisk well to form a dressing.

Divide the greens equally among 4 salad plates and top with the lotus root slices. Drizzle the dressing evenly over each and serve.

Celery Root Rémoulade

SERVES 4 OR 5

1/2 cup homemade or prepared mayonnaise

2 tablespoons Dijon or other French-style mustard

1 tablespoon white wine vinegar

1 small to medium-sized celery root, about
    3/4 pound

salt to taste

This is one of the great salads of simple French cooking. Usually served as a first course, either on its own or as a part of a collection of simple salads or raw vegetables, the crunchy texture and intense celery flavor of grated celery root, napped in a light dressing of mustard and mayonnaise, is utterly delicious. Indeed, it is so popular in France, that one can buy bags of ready-grated celery root in the produce department of most markets.

In a bowl large enough to accommodate the celery root eventually, combine the mayonnaise, mustard, and vinegar. Using a whisk or fork, beat thoroughly to make a creamy sauce. Taste and adjust the seasoning, adding salt if desired.

With a paring knife, peel the celery root. Grate it on the large holes of a hand-held grater.

Drain the celery root in a sieve and then thoroughly pat dry. Add it to the bowl of sauce and turn it to coat well. Serve slightly chilled or at room temperature.

Grated Carrot and Medjool Date Salad with Gorgonzola Dressing

The sharp, salty character of Gorgonzola and the natural sweetness of carrots and dates together create a delicious explosion of perfectly suited flavors. Although this is a salad that can be served to accompany a main dish, I prefer to savor it on its own as an appetizer, garnished with a few dandelion greens and plain water crackers.

SERVES 2 OR 3

Using a vegetable peeler or paring knife, peel the carrots. Grate them on the large holes of a hand-held grater to make 1 cup. Set aside. Chop the dates into pieces about the size of corn kernels and set them aside as well.

In a bowl, combine the cheese, olive oil, vinegar, and pepper, mashing and whisking the cheese to make a thick dressing. Add the carrots and the dates to the dressing and turn them until they are well coated.

Transfer to a serving bowl or to individual salad plates and garnish with dandelion, arugula, or lettuce. Serve at once.

3 or 4 carrots, about $1/2$ pound in all

4 dried Medjool dates, pitted

3 tablespoons firmly packed crumbled
Gorgonzola, Maytag or other blue cheese

$1/4$ cup olive oil

2 tablespoons Champagne vinegar or white
wine vinegar

$1/2$ teaspoon cracked black pepper

dandelion, arugula, or young lettuce leaves
for garnish

Soups and Stews

Roots conjure images of the hearty, slow-simmering soups and stews of fall and winter. And rightly so. The flavors of carrots, potatoes, parsnips, leeks, rutabagas, and turnips evolve and mellow as they simmer with sinewy cuts of meat, grains, and mushrooms. The broths develop enticing complexity from the roots during the long cooking, adding to the pleasure of "bread dipping." Springtime soups and stews made with the young roots of the season are equally flavorful. The young radishes, early green shoots of garlic and leeks, and tiny turnips and carrots need only brief cooking, however. If overcooked, they will dissolve and their flavor will dissipate.

In choosing the roots for soups and stews, the cook becomes an artist. The palette is the characteristics of the roots, the canvas the finished dish. Too many turnips will spoil the broth. Too few leeks will make a bland soup. Beets will turn the whole dish red. Lotus root and daikon radish absorb flavors from the broth in which they are cooked, but rutabaga will dominate any dish if discretion is not employed. The starchy roots—potato, parsnip, parsley root, and taro—act as natural thickeners, and if mashed or puréed, can make the soup or broth as dense as you desire. In contrast, those with a higher water content—carrot, turnip, Jerusalem artichoke, celery root—won't contribute as much thickening.

Leek and Potato Soup

SERVES 2 OR 3

2 leeks

2 potatoes, any kind

1 tablespoon butter or olive oil

4 cups chicken broth

This is a soup to prepare when you have little time at hand, but do have an intense longing for something comforting and homemade to eat.

Slice all the whites and about 2 inches of the greens of the leeks into $1/2$-inch-thick rounds. Set them aside. Peel the potatoes, if you like, and cut the potatoes into bite-sized pieces.

In a saucepan over medium heat, melt the butter or warm the olive oil. Add the leeks and sauté until they began to change color slightly, 2 to 3 minutes. Add the potatoes and cook for another minute or two, always stirring. Add the chicken broth and bring to a boil. Reduce the heat to low, cover, and simmer until the potatoes are tender but still hold their shape, about 20 minutes.

Ladle into warmed soup plates and serve at once.

Provençal Beef and Carrot Daube

When you make this stew, think of high plateaus and a windswept landscape, and of the kitchen made cozy all the cold day with the scent of beef simmering in wine laced with handfuls of wild herbs. By nightfall, the dark, rich stew is ready to be ladled atop wide noodles, coating them with its sauce. • This is a dish that requires a slightly tough cut of beef, as the same connective tissues that make meat tough also thicken and enrich the sauce. The longer and slower the cooking, the more tender the meat and flavorful the sauce. • A daube is one of those dishes that tastes even better the day after it is made. Some fierce traditionalists even insist that a daube can be served only after having allowed the flavors to merge for twenty-four hours.

In a large, heavy-bottomed Dutch oven or other stove-top casserole with a snug-fitting lid, warm the olive oil over medium heat. Add the garlic and onion and sauté them, stirring often, until the onion is barely translucent, 3 or 4 minutes. Add the meat, raise the heat to medium-high, and cook, turning the meat over as needed, until the pieces are browned on all sides, about 8 minutes. Remove the meat with a slotted spoon and set it aside.

Put the carrots in the same pan in which the meat was browned and cook them over medium heat, turning them in the pan juices, for 2 or 3 minutes. Return the meat to the pan and sprinkle the meat and carrots with the flour, salt, pepper, and dried thyme leaves or fresh sprigs. Continue to cook, turning the meat and carrots as needed to prevent burning, until the flour is browned, 2 or 3 minutes more. Remove the meat and carrots with a slotted spoon and set aside. Pour about one-third of the wine into the pan and, using a wooden spoon, scrape up any browned bits clinging to the pan bottom. Gradually add the remaining wine and bring it to a boil. Reduce the heat to low and simmer for 5 minutes to blend the ingredients.

Return the meat and carrots to the pot, cover, and simmer over the lowest possible heat, turning occasionally, for $2^{1}/2$ to 3 hours. Add the water during cooking if needed to thin the sauce a bit. The cooking time will depend upon the toughness of the meat used, but the principle is that when the meat is almost tender enough to cut with a fork and shreds can be pulled from it, it is almost done. The sauce should be thick enough to coat the back of a spoon briefly.

When the meat and sauce have reached this stage, uncover and cook until the meat is tender enough to cut easily with a fork, another 35 to 45 minutes. As this point, remove the daube from the heat, allow it to cool, and then refrigerate overnight, if possible, before reheating and serving. Five minutes before serving, stir in the fresh thyme.

SERVES 6

2 tablespoons olive oil

3 garlic cloves, chopped

1 large yellow onion, chopped

2 pounds boneless beef chuck, cut into
    $2^{1}/2$-inch pieces

6 to 8 carrots, unpeeled, cut into 1-inch pieces

2 tablespoons all-purpose flour

1 teaspoon salt

1 teaspoon freshly ground black pepper

1 tablespoon dried thyme leaves, or 3 or 4
    fresh thyme sprigs, each about 6 inches
    long

2 cups dry red wine such as Burgundy or
    Merlot

$1/2$ to 1 cup water, if needed

1 tablespoon chopped fresh thyme

Lamb Stew with Sweet Potatoes, Poblano Chilies, and Pomegranate

The sweet potatoes and chilies are cooked separately, then added to the simmered lamb and its boldly seasoned broth, along with pomegranate juice and seeds, five minutes before serving. Accompany the stew with a crunchy grain such as bulgur or brown rice.

Serves 4 to 6

Cut the sweet potatoes crosswise into 1 1/2-inch-thick slices. Place the slices on a steamer rack over boiling water, cover, and steam until they are tender enough to be pierced with the tines of a fork, about 30 minutes. Remove from the rack, and when cool enough to handle, peel the pieces and set them aside. Alternatively, boil the sweet potato slices in water to cover generously until tender, about 30 minutes, then drain and peel.

Meanwhile, preheat a broiler or prepare a charcoal or gas grill. Place the chilies on a broiler pan or the grill rack and broil or grill until the skins are charred and blistered, 2 to 3 minutes on each side. Place the peppers in a plastic bag or wrap them in a towel to sweat for about 5 minutes. Slit the peppers lengthwise and remove the stems and seeds. Using your fingers, peel off the skins. Cut the chilies lengthwise into 1/2-inch-wide strips and set aside. Cut the pomegranate in half and, using your fingers, remove enough of the seeds to measure 1/4 cup. This will be approximately one-fourth of the total seeds. Using a juice extractor or reamer, extract the juice from the pomegranate halves (even though some seeds are missing). Strain the juice to remove any bits of white pith, as they will make the juice bitter. Set the seeds and juice aside.

In a deep, heavy-bottomed saucepan over medium heat, warm the olive oil. Add the garlic and sauté for a minute or two. Add the lamb and sauté, stirring often, until it has browned on all sides, 7 or 8 minutes.

Sprinkle the flour, turmeric, cumin, salt, and cayenne pepper over the meat and turn the meat as needed to brown the flour and spices, 3 or 4 minutes. Halve the lemon and squeeze the juice over the contents of the pan. Using a wooden spoon, scrape up any browned bits stuck to the pan bottom. Add the chicken broth and water, reduce the heat to low, and simmer, uncovered, until the lamb is tender, about 1 hour.

When the lamb is done, add the sweet potatoes, chili strips, and the pomegranate juice and seeds. Simmer for about 5 minutes, then serve.

1 1/2 pounds yellow- or orange-fleshed
    sweet potatoes, unpeeled

3 fresh poblano chilies

1 pomegranate

1 tablespoon olive oil

2 garlic cloves, crushed

1 pound lean boneless lamb, cut into
    1-inch pieces

1 tablespoon all-purpose flour

1 teaspoon ground turmeric

1/2 teaspoon ground cumin

1/4 teaspoon salt

1/2 teaspoon cayenne pepper

1 lemon

1 cup chicken broth

1 cup water

soups and stews

Spring Lamb and Young Root Ragout

This stew, made with the first young vegetables of spring, is a seasonal celebration of the garden. Unlike the long-simmering stews of winter, this one cooks quickly, as the vegetables are immature and still very tender and thus have no need for the long cooking that fully mature roots require.

8 baby-sized turnips

$1/2$ to $3/4$ pound green peas

$1/2$ to $3/4$ pound fava beans

6 young leeks

2 tablespoons butter

1 pound lamb sirloin or other tender cut,
   cubed into 1-inch pieces

1 tablespoon all-purpose flour

$1/2$ teaspoon salt

1 teaspoon freshly ground black pepper

$1/2$ cup dry white wine

$1 1/2$ cups chicken or vegetable broth

12 to 14 small new potatoes, about
   $1 1/4$ pounds in all, unpeeled

14 to 16 small, young carrots, unpeeled

2 tablespoons minced fresh chives

1 tablespoon minced fresh tarragon

1 tablespoon minced fresh parsley

Trim the turnips, leaving about $1/2$-inch of their greens attached. Place the turnips in a steamer rack over boiling water, cover, and steam until they are tender enough to be pierced with the tip of a knife, 8 to 10 minutes. Shell the peas and set them aside. You should have a little more than $1/2$ cup. Shell the fava beans. Unless they are very young and garden fresh, peel them as well; the skin can render them strong tasting and they will seem out of place in this delicately flavored dish. The skins are easily removed by slitting them with the tip of a knife and slipping them off. Steam the peas and favas on a rack over boiling water until a sampled one is tender to the bite, 6 or 7 minutes. Alternatively, parboil them in water to cover until tender as above, then drain. Set the favas and peas aside.

Cut the whites and pale tender greens of the leeks into 2-inch lengths. You will have about 12 pieces. Chop enough of the remaining tender green tops to measure $1/4$ cup. Set the leeks and the leek greens aside.

In a large, heavy-bottomed Dutch oven or other stove-top casserole, melt the butter over medium heat. When it foams, add the lamb and sauté, turning as needed, until the meat is lightly colored on all sides, 5 or 6 minutes. Sprinkle the flour, salt, and pepper over the lamb and continue to cook, stirring often, until the flour has turned quite brown, 3 or 4 minutes. Increase the heat to high. Pour in the white wine and, using a wooden spoon, scrape up any browned bits stuck to the bottom of the pan. Add about half of the broth and continue to stir until all the bits are scraped up and incorporated into the liquid. Add the rest of the broth and the potatoes. Cover with a tightly fitting lid, reduce the heat to medium-low, and simmer for 10 minutes.

Stir in the carrots and the chopped leek greens and layer the leek pieces on top. Cover and cook until the carrots and potatoes are tender when pierced with the tip of a sharp knife, another 8 to 10 minutes. Add the turnips, peas, and favas, turning them gently in the simmering stew. Cover and cook for 2 or 3 minutes longer, just long enough for the flavors to incorporate. If you want a thicker stew, scoop out 1 or 2 potatoes, plus a little broth, purée them together in a blender or a food processor, and stir them back in.

Taste for salt, adding more if desired, then stir in all but about 1 teaspoon of each of the herbs. Serve the ragout sprinkled with the remaining herbs.

Fall Garden Minestrone

SERVES 6 TO 8 AS A MAIN DISH

Versions of minestrone vary not only from cook to cook but also from season to season, yet roots nearly always play a role. In winter, carrots and keeper potatoes are significant, along with broccoli, canned Italian plum tomatoes, dried cannellini or cranberry beans, and sturdy *cavolo nero,* the wonderful Italian black cabbage that is actually a long, strap-leaved savoyed kale. Springtime finds the soup plumped with tiny new potatoes, fresh shelled peas, and tender carrots and turnips, but for me fall is the ideal season to make this thick, rich vegetable soup. The last of summer's ripe tomatoes and squashes can be combined with fall's tender fennel, early turnips, shell beans, and first cabbage, as well as freshly dug potatoes.

1/4 cup olive oil

2 tablespoons butter

1 yellow or white onion, chopped

2 garlic cloves, chopped

4 medium-sized potatoes, preferably Yukon Gold
or other waxy type, chopped (about 5 cups)

4 baby fennel bulbs, plus 3 inches of stalk, chopped

2 cups mixed snap beans such as Romano, Blue
Lake, and yellow wax, in any combination

2 small to medium-sized zucchini, chopped

2 cups coarsely chopped black cabbage (Lacinato kale)
or green cabbage

3/4 to 1 pound fresh cranberry or other shell
beans, shelled

2 cups peeled and coarsely chopped ripe tomatoes

6 cups chicken, beef, or vegetable broth

2 tablespoons chopped fresh marjoram or oregano

rind piece of Parmesan or Romano cheese (optional)

salt and freshly ground black pepper

freshly grated Parmesan cheese for garnish (optional)

Put the olive oil and butter in a large soup pot over medium heat. When the butter foams, add the onion and garlic. Sauté for 2 or 3 minutes, then add the potatoes and sauté for 2 or 3 minutes longer. Continue this process, adding the vegetables, except the shell beans, one at a time in the order given and then sautéing each one for 2 or 3 minutes before adding the next. Once the tomatoes have been added, pour in the broth. Bring to a boil over high heat, then reduce the heat to low and cover the soup pot. Cook, stirring occasionally, for 2 hours. The soup should be rather thick at this point. Add the shell beans, the marjoram or oregano, and the cheese rind, if using. Cook until the shell beans are tender, 30 to 40 minutes.

Taste for salt and pepper. Ladle into bowls and serve piping hot, garnished with grated Parmesan, if desired.

Salt cod is popular in Mediterranean countries during winter, the same time that hardy roots and kale are in season. The rutabaga here is particularly good, as the other flavors are powerful enough to welcome its contribution rather than be overwhelmed by it.

SERVES 4

To refresh the salt cod, soak the fillets in a large amount of cold water for about 15 minutes, then drain the water and repeat the process 3 times, to equal 1 hour of soaking, the minimum needed. The length of time needed to refresh salt cod varies, however, and can range from 1 hour to overnight, depending upon the amount of salt in the fish and how dry it is. The fish should be a little salty—that is part of its character—but not unpleasantly so. Conversely, it should not be devoid of all its salt, and oversoaking will do that. To check the saltiness, cut off a small piece, simmer it in water for 2 or 3 minutes, and taste it. If it is very salty after 1 hour of soaking, let soak in clean water 6 hours and retest. If still quite salty, let soak in yet another bath of clean water for 3 to 6 hours. It may seem tedious, but adding salt cod to one's fish repertoire is well worth experimenting with refreshing it. When ready, cut the fish into 1/2-inch squares and set aside.

In a deep, heavy-bottomed saucepan over medium heat, warm the olive oil. Add the garlic and onion and sauté until translucent, 3 or 4 minutes. Sprinkle on the cumin, saffron, and black pepper. Stir for a minute, then add a little broth and the water and stir to mix well. Add the remaining broth and bring to a boil. Reduce the heat to low and simmer, uncovered, for about 30 minutes.

Meanwhile, using a vegetable peeler or paring knife, peel the rutabagas. Then, if you like, peel the potatoes as well. Cut the potatoes and rutabagas into 1-inch cubes. When the broth has simmered for 30 minutes, add the potatoes, rutabagas, tomatoes, and olives. Cover and simmer until the vegetables are almost tender, about 30 minutes. They should offer some resistance when pierced with the tines of a fork.

Add the peas and chili and simmer for another few minutes before adding the cod, kale, oregano, and thyme. Cover and simmer for a final 4 or 5 minutes, or until the cod is just cooked and flakes when pulled apart with a fork; overcooking will make it tough.

Taste and adjust with salt, then serve immediately.

1/2 pound salt cod fillets

1 tablespoon olive oil

2 garlic cloves, minced

1 yellow or white onion, coarsely chopped

2 teaspoons ground cumin

1 teaspoon saffron threads

1 teaspoon freshly ground black pepper

4 cups chicken or vegetable broth

1 cup water

2 small rutabagas, about 1/3 pound in all

3 medium-sized potatoes, either baking type such as Russet or waxy type such as Yukon Gold, about 1 pound in all

1/2 cup chopped plum tomatoes with their juice

12 Kalamata olives

1/2 pound green peas, shelled (about 1/2 cup)

2 tablespoons minced dried red chili such as Anaheim or Colorado

1 cup chopped kale

1 tablespoon chopped fresh oregano

1 tablespoon chopped fresh thyme

soups and stews

Creamy Clam and Celery Root Chowder

SERVES 4

Using celery root, which is low in starch, instead of the traditional potatoes gives the chowder a light character and lively flavor.

2 cans (6¹/2 ounces each) chopped clams
   and their juice, or 1¹/2 cups freshly
   shucked clams and their liquor

1 medium-sized celery root, about ³/4 pound

2 tablespoons butter

¹/2 cup minced yellow or white onion

1 celery stalk and leaves, chopped

2 tablespoons all-purpose flour

2 cups milk

1 teaspoon red pepper flakes

salt to taste

Drain the clams and set them aside, reserving the clam liquid and adding enough water to equal 2 cups. Using a paring knife, peel the celery root, then chop it into 1/2-inch cubes. You should have about 1 1/4 cups.

In a heavy-bottomed saucepan over medium heat, melt the butter. Add the onion, celery stalk and leaves, and celery root. Sauté until the onion and celery are translucent and the celery root begins to change color a bit, 3 or 4 minutes. Sprinkle the flour over the vegetables and sauté for another 1 or 2 minutes, then add the reserved clam liquid slowly, stirring as you go. Leaving the pan uncovered, reduce the heat to low and simmer until the celery root is tender, 8 to 10 minutes. With the back of a wooden spoon, mash some of the celery root to thicken the soup.

In the meantime, in a saucepan, heat the milk until very hot—scalding—but not boiling. When the celery root is tender, add the clams and cook for 2 or 3 minutes. Pour in the hot milk, and add the red pepper flakes. Mix well, taste for salt, and simmer for 1 to 2 minutes. Ladle into warmed bowls and serve piping hot.

Roast Corn, Red Pepper, and Jerusalem Artichoke Soup

grilling the corn and sweet red peppers before cooking them in the soup endows this dish with its smoky flavor—a flavor that marries perfectly with the hazelnut taste of the Jerusalem artichokes. Quick and simple to prepare, this soup can be ladled up as a main dish, a side dish to a sandwich, or a first course. Bits of cooked chicken or spicy sausage can be added to make a heartier soup, if desired.

SERVES 4

Prepare a charcoal or gas grill. Remove the husks and strip the silks from the corn and discard. Place the whole peppers and the ears of corn on the grill rack about 6 inches from the heat source. Grill the peppers, turning often, until the skins are black and blistered. Lightly brown the ears of corn, turning often. The kernels should be barely golden and have begun to shrivel a bit.

Remove the peppers and corn from the grill. Place the peppers in a plastic bag or wrap them in a towel to sweat for about 5 minutes. Slit the peppers lengthwise and remove the stems and seeds. Using your fingers, peel off the skins. Cut the peppers into $1/2$-inch dice and set them aside.

Working with 1 ear of corn at a time, hold the ear upright, thicker end down, in a bowl. Using a sharp knife, scrape off the kernels into a bowl in a downward cut. You will notice the corn is milky; by removing the kernels this way, you will be able to capture some of that milk, which helps give the soup its flavor. Set the bowl of kernels aside.

Using a paring knife, peel the Jerusalem artichokes and dice them into pieces just a bit larger than the peppers. You will need $2 1/2$ cups. Reserve any extra for another use.

If using the bacon, cut it into small pieces and put it in a heavy-bottomed saucepan or soup pot. Place over medium-low heat until the bacon shrinks and is cooked through, 3 or 4 minutes. If using the olive oil, simply warm it in the pan or pot. Add the onion and celery, raise the heat to medium, and sauté until the onion is translucent, 3 to 4 minutes. Add the Jerusalem artichokes and continue to cook, stirring, for another 2 to 3 minutes. Add the corn, sweet pepper, broth, water, salt, and pepper. Reduce the heat to low and simmer until the Jerusalem artichokes are tender to the bite, 10 to 15 minutes. Stir in the thyme and oregano and simmer for another minute or two.

Taste for salt and add more if desired. Ladle into warmed bowls and serve piping hot.

4 ears white or yellow sweet corn

2 large red sweet peppers

3 or 4 small Jerusalem artichokes, about 1 pound in all

5 slices bacon, or $1/4$ cup olive oil

$1/2$ yellow or white onion, minced

$2/3$ cup chopped celery

3 cups chicken or vegetable broth

1 cup water

1 teaspoon salt

1 teaspoon freshly ground black pepper

2 tablespoons minced fresh thyme

2 tablespoons minced fresh oregano

soups and stews

This is an old-fashioned farm-style barley soup, made earthy with bits of rutabaga and slivers of spinach. Other roots can, of course, be used instead of, or in combination with, the rutabaga. I find this to be a good soup for lunch, served along with grilled bread rubbed with olive oil and topped with just a sprinkle of Parmesan cheese.

SERVES 4 OR 5

In a saucepan, combine the barley and water and bring to a boil. Reduce the heat to low, cover, and cook until tender to the bite, 1 to 1¹/2 hours. Remove from the heat, drain, and set aside.

In a large saucepan or a soup pot over medium heat, melt the butter. Add the leek and rutabaga and sauté until the leek begins to change color, 3 or 4 minutes. Add the broth and water and bring to a boil over high heat. Reduce the heat to low and simmer, uncovered, until the rutabaga is tender, 15 to 20 minutes.

Remove from the heat and let cool slightly. In a blender or food processor, roughly purée half of the soup and then return it to the saucepan. Add the reserved barley, the half-and-half, milk, and spinach and place over medium heat. Bring to a simmer and simmer just long enough for the soup to be piping hot and to wilt the spinach.

Ladle into warmed bowls and serve at once.

¹/4 cup pearl barley

3 cups water

¹/2 teaspoon salt

2 tablespoons butter

1 leek, including tender greens, minced

1 small rutabaga, peeled and finely diced

4 cups beef or vegetable broth

2 cups water

¹/2 cup half-and-half

¹/2 cup milk

1 cup julienned, stemmed spinach

Borscht with Horseradish Cream

4 medium to large red beets with leaves
   attached, 1¹/2 to 2 pounds in all

1 cup chopped beet leaves

4 cups beef or vegetable broth

1 white or yellow onion, minced

1 carrot, peeled and minced

2 large celery stalks, minced

2 tomatoes, peeled, seeded and chopped

¹/2 teaspoon salt

¹/2 teaspoon freshly ground black pepper

¹/4 cup freshly grated horseradish

¹/2 cup sour cream

¹/2 cup chopped fresh dill

borscht is one of the classics of northern European country cooking, and its versions vary not only from country to country, but also from region to region. Some include beef; others are meatless. Usually the borscht is served with a dollop of cold sour cream and a healthy sprinkling of fresh dill on top. They are my favorite part. The result is a taste sensation balanced between the stolid beets and the soaring lightness of the cold cream and sprightly dill. In this version, a little fresh horseradish root is incorporated into the sour cream. Accompany with thick slices of black country bread and butter.

Cut off all but 1 inch of the beet tops. Reserve the youngest, most tender leaves to incorporate into the soup; chop them to measure 1 cup and set aside. Place the beets in a saucepan with enough water to cover by 2 or 3 inches. Bring to a boil, cover, reduce the heat to low, and simmer until tender when pierced with the tip of a sharp knife and the skins will slip off easily, 45 minutes to 1¹/4 hours; the timing will depend upon the size and maturity of the beets. Alternatively, place the trimmed beets on a steamer rack over boiling water, cover, and steam until tender, about 1¹/4 hours.

While the beets are cooking, place the broth, onion, carrot, celery, chopped beet leaves, tomatoes, salt, and pepper in a heavy-bottomed saucepan or soup pot. Place over medium heat and bring to a boil. Reduce the heat to low, partially cover, and simmer until the vegetables and onions are tender and the broth has absorbed some of their flavor, about 30 minutes. Taste for salt, and add as desired.

When the beets are done, drain them (or remove them from the steamer rack) and let stand until they are cool enough to handle, then slip off the skins with your fingers or use a paring knife. They may now be cut into bite-sized chunks, slices, or julienned. The last presents a more refined version, while the chunks are more country style. You should have about 2 cups beets. Add these to the broth and simmer for another 10 minutes.

In a small bowl, stir together the horseradish and sour cream.

To serve, ladle the hot soup into bowls. Top with a spoonful of horseradish cream and a sprinkling of chopped dill. Serve at once.

Lotus Root in Two-Mushroom Broth

SERVES 4

Thin slices of lotus root floating atop a clear broth show off the root's elegant cut-lace pattern to best advantage.

3 or 4 dried shiitake mushrooms

1 cup boiling water

1/4 pound fresh shiitake mushrooms,
   brushed clean

3 green onions, including tender greens,
   cut into 2-inch lengths

1 carrot, unpeeled, cut into 2-inch lengths

1-inch piece fresh ginger, sliced, plus
   4 teaspoons grated

1/4 cup dry sherry

1 star anise

3 1/2 cups chicken broth

1 small lotus root, about 1/2 pound

ice water, as needed

1/2 teaspoon soy sauce (optional)

4 tablespoons chopped fresh cilantro

Put the dried mushrooms in a bowl and pour the boiling water over them. Let stand until softened, about 20 minutes. Squeeze the mushrooms to release all the moisture from them and then chop them. Set aside. Strain the mushroom-infused water through a sieve lined with cheesecloth. There should be approximately 3/4 cup liquid. Set the liquid aside. Set aside 1 large fresh shiitake mushroom and quarter the remaining mushrooms, including the stems. Place the green onions, carrot, sliced ginger, sherry, star anise, the reserved mushroom liquid, chopped dried mushrooms, quartered fresh mushrooms, and chicken broth in a saucepan. Place over medium-high heat and bring to a boil. Reduce the heat to medium-low, cover, and simmer for 35 minutes.

While the broth is cooking, prepare the lotus root by removing the skin with a paring knife and cutting the root crosswise into scant 1/4-inch-thick slices. You will need about 16 slices for the soup, 4 slices per serving. Place the slices in a bowl of ice water to keep them crisp until ready to use.

When the broth has finished simmering, remove the saucepan from the heat and strain the broth through a fine-mesh sieve, discarding the spent vegetables and spice. Return the broth to a clean saucepan. Drain the lotus root and add to the broth. Slice the reserved fresh shiitake into paper-thin slices and add these to the broth as well. Bring the broth to a shimmering simmer over medium heat, then reduce the heat to low and simmer for 5 minutes. Taste for seasoning, adding the soy sauce, if desired.

Ladle into bowls, dividing the lotus root and mushroom slices evenly. Garnish each bowl with a teaspoon of grated ginger and a tablespoon of chopped cilantro and serve.

SERVES 4

Smooth and creamy, yet intensely flavored, this is a soup for a cozy winter night, either as a main dish or an appetizing first course to a special meal.

With a vegetable peeler or paring knife, peel the parsley roots, then cut them into $1/2$-inch pieces. You should have between 12 and 15 pieces. Set aside. In a small bowl, using the back of a wooden spoon, cream together 1 tablespoon of the butter and the flour until the flour is thoroughly incorporated into the butter. Set it aside as well.

Put the broth and water in a heavy-bottomed saucepan and add the parsley roots. Place over medium heat and bring to a boil. Reduce to medium-low and simmer, uncovered, for 5 minutes. Add the 4 cups watercress and the butter-flour mixture and simmer until the parsley roots are tender when pierced with the tip of a sharp knife, another 5 to 10 minutes. Stir in the nutmeg, salt, and pepper.

Remove from the heat and let cool slightly. In a blender or food processor, working in batches if necessary, purée the soup until smooth. Add the cream and process until combined. The soup will be a lovely pale green. Pour it into a clean saucepan and place over medium heat. Bring to a simmer. Meanwhile, melt the remaining 1 tablespoon butter in a small skillet over medium heat. When it foams, add the bread crumbs and toss to coat them and heat them through.

Ladle the soup into warmed bowls. Garnish with the watercress sprigs and the hot, toasty bread crumbs and serve piping hot.

5 or 6 parsley roots, about $1/3$ pound

2 tablespoons butter

2 tablespoons all-purpose flour

3 cups chicken broth

1 cup water

4 cups watercress, including tender stems, plus 4 watercress sprigs for garnish

$1/4$ teaspoon freshly grated nutmeg

$1/2$ teaspoon salt

$1/2$ teaspoon white pepper (or freshly ground black pepper if you don't mind the dark specks)

$1/4$ cup heavy cream

$1/4$ cup fresh bread crumbs

soups and stews

Pot au Feu

SERVES 6 TO 8

FOR THE MEAT AND THE BROTH:

5 quarts water

1 tablespoon salt

8 black peppercorns

2 dried bay leaves, or 4 fresh bay leaves

8 fresh parsley sprigs, each 4 inches long

8 fresh thyme sprigs, each 4 inches long

1 beef brisket, 4 to 5 pounds

3 celery stalks

3 leeks, including tender greens, cut into
   4-inch lengths

3 carrots, unpeeled, halved crosswise

2 large white or yellow onions, halved

Root vegetables are in their glory in this French classic. First, carrots, leeks, onions, celery, and a bouquet garni are simmered along with the beef brisket, which becomes flavorful and moist during the long, slow cooking required to produce the broth. These vegetables, having yielded their essence to the liquid, are then discarded. New roots, these to be served with the meat, are added and the cooking continues until both the meat and vegetables are tender. To serve, the meat is removed from the broth and cut into slices, which are then arranged on a platter and surrounded by the second batch of vegetables. Sauces of mustard, mayonnaise, and horserad-ish and relishes of pickled fruits and vegetables are set out as accompaniments. The broth is saved for the next day, when pasta is added to make a rich soup. Any leftovers from the previ-ous day's platter may be chopped and added to the pot and the resulting soup can be served topped with freshly grated Parmesan cheese.

For the meat and broth, combine the water, salt, and peppercorns in a soup pot large enough to hold the meat and vegetables comfortably. Tie the bay leaves and the parsley and thyme sprigs together with kitchen string to make a bouquet garni (or they can be added untied, since the whole broth will eventually be strained). Add to the pot along with the meat, celery stalks, leeks, carrots, and onions. Bring to a boil over high heat and cook for 3 or 4 minutes at a rolling boil. A surface scum will collect as the meat cooks and this should be skimmed off. Reduce the heat to low, cover with the lid ajar, and simmer until the meat is tender and shreds easily when pulled with a fork, $2^{1}/2$ to 3 hours. Continue to skim the surface of any scum during this time. At the end of the cooking period, when the meat is tender, you should have about $2^{1}/2$ quarts broth in which to cook the vegetables for the final dish.

To make the final dish, remove the meat from the soup pot and set aside. Line a sieve with cheesecloth or use a very fine-mesh sieve. Strain the broth through the sieve and discard the contents of the sieve. Skim off any fat and discard. Return about 2^1/$_2$ quarts (10 cups) of the broth to a clean soup pot. Add all the vegetables and bring to a boil over high heat. Reduce the heat to low and cover the pot. Simmer for 25 minutes, then return the meat to the pot, spooning the broth over it. Cover tightly and simmer for another 10 minutes, then remove the cover. Continue to simmer until all the vegetables can be easily pierced with a fork but still hold their shape, about 10 minutes longer.

Remove the meat to a serving platter. Using a slotted spoon, scoop out all the vegetables. Reserve the broth for next day's pasta. Serve the meat and vegetables as suggested in the headnote. Alternatively, the meat slices and vegetables may be served in soup plates with a ladle of broth poured over each serving.

FOR THE FINAL DISH:

2^1/$_2$ quarts reserved broth

2 leeks, whites and tender greens, cut into
    2-inch lengths

6 small white boiling onions or 3 small yellow
    onions, quartered lengthwise

3 small turnips, peeled and halved, or 6 baby
    turnips, unpeeled and left whole

2 medium-sized rutabagas, peeled and
    quartered

4 medium-sized boiling potatoes such as
    Red Rose or White Rose, peeled, if desired,
    and halved

4 medium-sized parsnips, peeled and cut into
    2-inch lengths

4 carrots, peeled and cut into 2-inch lengths

Main Dishes

Main dishes are the centerpiece of a meal. In these, roots may be the primary element, a complement, or the seasoning accent that defines the dish. Whole roasted onions stuffed with sausage and bread, a savory onion or leek tart, and shepherd's pie with its topping of mashed potatoes all star the root. An array of different roots, or a single type such as turnips, tucked around a beef or pork roast, a plump chicken, or game hens, absorb some of the roasting juices and thus become integrated into the whole. Roots may be equal partners with meat or other vegetables in a stir-fry or a baked dish, or provide only the flavoring element. A chicken whose flesh has been infused with the fragrance of garlic while cooking will be quite different from one that has steeped overnight in a ginger-based sauce.

glistening golden brown, surrounded by glazed turnips and their wilted greens, this dish makes a dazzling table presentation. Use only young, tender greens; more mature ones are too powerful for the brief cooking. The flavors dazzle as well, as each bite of the deliciously rich duck marries with the sweetness of the grapes and the mild pungency of the young turnips and tender greens.

SERVES 3 OR 4

Preheat an oven to 425 degrees F.

Remove the giblets from the duck and set aside. Rinse the duck and pat dry. Using a needle, pierce the skin a dozen times to help draw off the fat as the duck cooks. Rub the duck all over with the salt and pepper. Stick the cloves in the onion pieces and tuck them into the duck cavity, along with the giblets and sage sprigs. Put the duck, breast up, on a rack in an uncovered roasting pan and roast for 50 minutes.

Using a paring knife, peel the turnips and then quarter them lengthwise. Place on a steamer rack over boiling water, cover, and steam until tender when pierced with the tip of a sharp knife, 10 to 15 minutes. Remove from the rack and set aside.

Remove the roasting pan from the oven and set the duck and rack aside. Pour off all the juices but 1 tablespoon and replace the rack and the duck, breast up, in the pan. Place the cooked turnips in the roasting pan with the duck and turn them to coat them with the pan juices. Add three-fourths of the grapes and all of the chopped greens, turning them also. Return the pan to the oven and continue to roast, uncovered, turning the turnips and greens several times, until the turnips are slightly golden and the greens wilted but still brightly colored, another 10 to 15 minutes. Remove from the oven and let stand, loosely covered with aluminum foil, for 10 minutes before carving.

Place the duck on a warmed serving platter. Surround it with the turnips, greens, and grapes. Garnish with small clusters of the remaining grapes. Carve at the table.

1 duck, 3¹/2 to 4 pounds

1/2 teaspoon salt

1/2 teaspoon freshly ground black pepper

12 whole cloves

2 white or yellow onions, quartered

4 fresh sage sprigs

4 medium-sized turnips, about 1 pound in all

1/2 cup Zante (Champagne) grapes or other larger sweet grapes, halved

2 cups chopped young turnip greens or mustard greens

main dishes

Beef Shanks and Pan-Roasted Parsnips

4 slices beef shanks, each about 1 inch
   thick, about 2 pounds in all

$1/2$ teaspoon salt

$1/2$ teaspoon freshly ground black pepper

3 or 4 parsnips, about $1^1/2$ pounds in all,
   unpeeled

$1^1/2$ cups minced leeks, including tender
   greens (2 medium-sized or 5 baby-sized)

1 celery stalk, minced

1 tablespoon minced fresh rosemary

$1/2$ teaspoon pesticide-free dried lavender,
   or 1 tablespoon minced fresh thyme

$1/2$ cup dry red wine

$1^1/2$ cups beef broth

$1/4$ cup chopped fresh parsley

here, parsnips are introduced in two steps: Early in the cooking, they serve to thicken and enrich the braising juices with their natural sugars and create the sauce. During the last half hour of cooking more parsnips are added and these become the glossy, golden brown roots that are served alongside the shanks, with the sauce drizzled over all. Serve with fresh peas or steamed green beans to mingle on the plate.

Preheat an oven to 450 degrees F.

Sprinkle the shanks with the salt and pepper and place in a roasting pan just large enough to hold them in a single layer. Put them in the oven and roast for 20 to 25 minutes.

While the shanks are cooking, cut 1 to $1^1/2$ parsnips into 1-inch cubes to measure $1^1/2$ cups. Cut the remaining 2 or more parsnips in half lengthwise, then into wedges about $1/2$ inch thick. Set all the parsnips aside.

Remove the roasting pan from the oven and remove the shanks. Pour off the pan juices. Return the shanks to the pan, cover them with the leeks and celery, and tuck the parsnip wedges around the shanks. Add the rosemary and lavender or thyme and pour the wine and broth over all. Cover tightly with a lid or aluminum foil and return to the oven. Reduce the heat to 400 degrees F and cook for 45 minutes. Remove the cover and turn the shanks, ensuring that the vegetables are now in the sauce. Replace the cover and cook until the vegetables are very soft and the parsnips can be mashed with the back of a wooden spoon, another 15 to 20 minutes. The edges of the shanks will be curling up, but the meat will not yet be tender.

Remove the pan from the oven. Using a slotted spatula, carefully remove the shanks from the pan, keeping their bone and marrow intact, if possible. Set aside. Skim the fat from the sauce and discard. Strain the remaining sauce and reserve about $1^1/2$ cups. Return the shanks to the pan, place the reserved parsnip cubes around them, and pour the reserved sauce over all. Cover again and cook for another 30 minutes. Remove the cover and baste the shanks and parsnips with the sauce. Re-cover and cook until the parsnips and shanks are tender and easily pierced with tines of a fork, another 15 to 20 minutes.

To serve, spoon the shanks, with their bone and marrow intact, onto a warmed platter. Surround them with the parsnips and drizzle a little sauce over all. Garnish with the parsley and serve the remaining sauce alongside.

Sweet leeks and smoky ham were made for each other. Bound together in a light sauce of white Cheddar and topped with toasty bread crumbs, they transform this simple gratin into a party dish for brunch, lunch, or dinner by making it in individual ramekins to bring hot and bubbling to the table. Garnish with slices of fresh tomatoes in summer or fall, and slices of oranges in winter and spring.

SERVES 4

Preheat an oven to 375 degrees F.

Cut the whites of the leeks into bite-sized lengths, about 3/4 to 1 inch long. Using the end of the leek greens closest to the white portion, mince enough to make 1 cup and set aside.

Arrange the whites of the leeks on a steamer rack over gently boiling water. Cover and steam until the leeks are limp, 5 or 6 minutes. Remove from the steamer and set aside.

Using 1 tablespoon of the butter, grease 4 single-serving-sized ramekins or one 9-inch oval gratin dish or other baking dish.

To prepare the sauce, melt 2 tablespoons of the butter in a heavy-bottomed saucepan over medium heat. When the butter begins to foam, remove the pan from the heat and whisk in the flour, salt, nutmeg, and pepper until a paste forms. Return the pan to medium heat and gradually whisk in the milk in a steady stream. Reduce the heat to low and stir until there are no lumps. Then simmer the sauce uncovered, stirring occasionally, until it becomes thick enough to coat the back of a spoon, about 10 minutes.

Stir in half of the cheese and continue to cook only until the cheese has melted, 2 or 3 minutes. Stir in the minced leek greens. Taste for seasonings and adjust for salt, if necessary.

If you are using ramekins, place them on a baking sheet for ease of handling later. Arrange the white leek pieces in the bottoms of the ramekins or in the large baking dish, top with the ham, and then the remaining cheese. Pour the sauce evenly over the top, making sure it drizzles down and through the layers. Top with the bread crumbs. Cut the remaining 1/2 tablespoon butter into bits and dot them over the top. Bake until the surface is golden and slightly bubbling, 12 to 15 minutes. Remove from the oven and serve hot. If ramekins were used, place each one on a plate along with a garnish of tomato or orange slices.

4 large, 8 medium, or 24 baby-sized leeks

3 1/2 tablespoons butter

3 tablespoons all-purpose flour

1/2 teaspoon salt

1/4 teaspoon freshly grated nutmeg

1/2 teaspoon freshly ground black pepper

1 cup milk

1/2 cup crumbled white Cheddar cheese

1 pound good-quality smoked ham

fine dried bread crumbs

tomato or orange slices if baked in ramekins

main dishes

Stir-fry of Young Turnips, Pork, and Pea Shoots

20 very small (1 inch in diameter) turnips,
   with greens attached

3 tablespoons light oil such as canola

1 teaspoon Asian sesame oil

1 pound lean pork, cut into ¹/₂-inch cubes

1 garlic clove, minced

1 tablespoon soy sauce

4 cups pea shoots, or 2 cups sugar snap or
   Chinese peas

This is a dish to prepare with the tiniest turnips of early spring or fall. Their flesh and flavor is delicate, and they need only few minutes of cooking to render them tender and slightly golden. Shrimp, scallops, or beef can be used in lieu of the pork and if pea shoots (the tender leaves and tendrils of the English pea plant, *Pisum sativum*) are unavailable, sugar snap or Chinese peas would be a good substitute. Serve with steamed white rice or noodles.

Cut off the greens to within ¹/₂ inch of the turnip. Reserve the young, tender, unblemished leaves to add to the stir-fry. Discard the others. Cut the turnips in half lengthwise.

In a wok or deep skillet over medium heat, combine the vegetable and sesame oils and heat until almost smoking. Add the turnips and stir-fry for 2 to 3 minutes, just until they have a tinge of gold. Remove to a plate and set aside.

Add the pork to the pan and stir-fry a minute or two until the meat becomes opaque. Remove the pork to the plate holding the turnips. Add the garlic and soy sauce to the pan and cook a few seconds until the garlic changes color slightly, then return the pork and turnips along with any collected juices to the pan. Stir-fry to mix well and add the pea shoots or peas and the reserved turnip leaves. Stir and turn all until the shoots change color slightly and become limp or the peas are crisp-tender, 1 to 3 minutes longer. Transfer to a serving dish and serve immediately.

Cooked lamb and potatoes quickly absorb the flavors of the mixed spices that comprise the curry flavoring, while the green peppers add a spicy bite of their own. Different root vegetables may be incorporated to create numerous versions of this home-style dish, all destined to be good. A topping of cool plain yogurt, sprinkled with chopped green herbs, completes the flavors. And if you have chutney on hand, do serve it.

Serves 4

In a heavy-bottomed skillet over medium heat, melt the butter. When it foams, add the onion and garlic and sauté until translucent, 1 to 2 minutes. Add the apple, carrot, and potatoes and sauté another 3 or 4 minutes, stirring often. Add the tomato, if using, and sauté for another minute. Sprinkle the turmeric, cumin, ground chili, salt, pepper, flour, and coriander over all. Continue to cook, stirring and turning the vegetables and coating them with the dry spices and flour, until the flour and spices begin to brown from the heat. Add about 1/4 cup of the broth, stirring as you pour until fully blended. Continue adding the remaining 1 3/4 cups broth slowly, stirring constantly, until it is all incorporated and has formed a sauce. This will take about 3 or 4 minutes.

Add the raisins, reduce the heat to low, and simmer, uncovered, until the carrots and potatoes are nearly tender when pierced with the tip of a sharp knife, and the sauce has thickened a bit, 15 to 20 minutes. Add the green pepper and cook for another 10 minutes. If the sauce becomes too thick, add a little more broth to thin it. Add the cooked lamb and heat through, another 3 or 4 minutes.

Serve hot, topped with a generous dollop of yogurt and a sprinkling of the fresh herbs.

4 tablespoons butter

1/2 yellow onion, minced

2 garlic cloves, minced

1 tart apple, peeled, cored, and chopped

1 carrot, chopped

8 small new or 3 medium-sized potatoes (any kind), peeled, if desired, and cut into 1-inch cubes

1 tomato, coarsely chopped (optional)

1 tablespoon ground turmeric

1 tablespoon ground cumin

1 tablespoon ground dried chili such as Anaheim, pasilla, or cayenne

1 teaspoon salt

1 teaspoon freshly ground black pepper

2 tablespoons all-purpose flour

6 coriander seeds, ground

2 cups chicken or vegetable broth, or as needed

1/4 cup raisins

1 large green bell pepper or other green sweet pepper, seeded and cut into 1-inch squares

1 1/2 cups cubed cooked lamb

1 cup plain yogurt

1 cup chopped fresh mint, tarragon, and chives, in equal amounts

main dishes

Horseradish-Salmon Cakes on Wilted Greens

MAKES 12 CAKES; SERVES 3 OR 4

*f*reshly grated horseradish mixed with the salmon adds loft and texture to the cakes, as well as imparting its inimitable flavor, in subdued form, to the whole. Small leaves of young spinach, red Asian mustard, or a mixture that includes young kale and red or green chard would be good choices for the greens. For lovers of horseradish, serve the cakes with Fresh Horseradish Sauce (page 47). This is an excellent next-day use of the leftovers from a whole poached salmon.

4 cups flaked poached salmon (about 1¹/2 pounds uncooked)

3 tablespoons grated onion, any kind

¹/2 cup freshly grated horseradish

2 tablespoons Dijon mustard

¹/2 cup chopped fresh flat-leaf parsley

2 eggs, beaten

1 teaspoon salt

2 teaspoons freshly ground black pepper

3 tablespoons vegetable oil

4 tablespoons butter

1¹/2 cups fine fresh bread crumbs seasoned with a little salt and pepper

6 cups greens (see headnote)

juice of 2 lemons

In a large bowl, combine the salmon, onion, horseradish, mustard, parsley, eggs, ¹/2 teaspoon of the salt, and the pepper. Using a fork, mash together all the ingredients until the mixture comes together in a mass that you can shape into balls. Form 12 balls. Each one will be about the size of a small lemon. Flatten into cakes approximately 2¹/2 inches in diameter. Set aside in a single layer on aluminum foil or waxed paper.

Preheat an oven to 300 degrees F.

Combine 1¹/2 tablespoons of the oil and 1¹/2 tablespoons of the butter in a skillet large enough to hold half of the cakes at one time. Place over medium heat. Meanwhile, sprinkle half of the bread crumbs onto another sheet of foil or waxed paper. Press both sides of 6 of the cakes into the crumbs. When the butter has melted, carefully slip the crumbed cakes into the skillet. Cook for about 2 minutes on each side until crispy brown. Remove and set aside to drain on absorbent towels or paper, then place in the oven to keep warm. Add the remaining 1¹/2 tablespoons oil and 1¹/2 tablespoons of the butter to the skillet, coat the remaining cakes with the remaining crumbs in the same manner, and then cook them as you did the first batch. Again, drain on absorbent towels and keep warm.

In a large skillet or wok over medium heat, melt the remaining 1 tablespoon butter. Add the greens, cover, and cook for 30 to 40 seconds. Uncover, stir, re-cover, and cook until the greens have just wilted but still retain their color, another 30 seconds. Sprinkle with the remaining ¹/2 teaspoon salt, increase the heat to high, and pour on the lemon juice. Stir and cook for another 15 to 20 seconds.

To serve, arrange a bed of the wilted greens on a platter or individual plates and top with the salmon cakes.

Poached Sea Bass on a Macédoine of Parsley Roots, Turnips, and Fennel

SERVES 4

Parsley root, fennel, and young, delicate turnips comprise this unusual version of macédoine, a classic composition of minced carrots, turnips, and flageolet beans. Sliced paper-thin and sautéed only moments in butter and white wine, the vegetables form a bed for the sea bass, which is covered with a tangle of fresh chervil and frisée as it quickly steams.

4 to 6 parsley roots, about 1/4 pound in all

12 small, young turnips, about 1 pound in all

1 fennel bulb, about 1/2 pound

1/2 tablespoon butter

1 pound sea bass or other firm white fish fillets, about 1/2 inch thick, cut into 4 equal pieces

1/2 teaspoon salt

1/2 cup torn fresh chervil sprigs (bite-sized pieces)

1/2 cup torn frisée, pale yellow portion only (bite-sized pieces)

1/3 cup dry white wine

With a vegetable peeler or a paring knife, peel the parsley roots. Cut them into wafer-thin slices. You should have about 1 cup. Trim the turnips, but do not peel. Slice them as you did the parsley roots. Again, you should have about 1 cup. Trim off the stems and any bruised areas from the fennel bulb and slice crosswise into wafer-thin slices. You should have about 3/4 cup. Set the parsley roots, turnips, and fennel aside.

Put the dinner plates in an oven preheated to 300 degrees F to warm them.

In a nonstick skillet just large enough to hold the fish in a single layer, melt the butter over medium heat. Increase the heat to medium-high and add the parsley roots, turnips, and fennel. Sauté them until they change color slightly and soften, 2 or 3 minutes. Place the pieces of fish on top of the vegetables. Sprinkle them with the salt and cook for 1 to 2 minutes. Then turn the fish and cook for about 1 minute on the other side. Top the fish with the chervil and frisée and add the white wine. Cover, reduce the heat to low, and cook until the fish is opaque and the chervil and frisée have wilted but still retain their color, another 2 minutes.

To serve, slide a spatula under each greens-topped fish fillet and its bed of vegetables and place on a warmed dinner plate.

a lovely browned crust forms on this dish as it cooks. When broken through to serve, layers of turnips that have all but dissolved into the cream are revealed, each of them punctuated by golden bits of sausage. The pungency of the turnips is mellowed as they simmer slowly in cream during cooking. Beets, or a combination of rutabagas and turnips, are equally successful in this deep-dish style.

SERVES 4 OR 5

Preheat an oven to 375 degrees F.

In a small bowl, combine the rosemary and half-and-half. Set it aside. The rosemary will infuse the cream. With a paring knife, peel the turnips. Cut them into 1/4-inch-thick rounds. You should have about 4 cups. Place the turnips on a steamer rack over boiling water, cover, and steam until they are easily pierced with the tip of a sharp knife, 10 to 15 minutes. Remove from the steamer rack and set aside.

Prick the sausages several times with the tines of a fork, then simmer them in a saucepan with water to cover for 5 minutes. Drain and then slice the sausages into 1-inch lengths. In a nonstick skillet over medium heat, melt 1 teaspoon of the butter. Add the sausage slices and cook, turning often, until they are lightly browned, 4 or 5 minutes. Remove the sausages to absorbent towels or paper to drain.

With 1 teaspoon of the remaining butter, grease an ovenproof baking dish that is just large enough to hold the turnips in several layers. A dish 3 to 4 inches deep and 9 or 10 inches square or round is perfect, but classic gratin dishes, which are shallower, will work as well.

Strain the half-and-half through a fine-mesh sieve placed over a small saucepan. Set the rosemary and the pan aside separately. Set aside 1/4 cup of the cheese for topping. Make a layer of about one-third of the turnip slices in the greased dish. Sprinkle with about one-third of the salt, pepper, and rosemary, and then top with half of the cheese and half of the sausage. Repeat the layers, ending with a layer of turnip slices topped with the seasonings. Sprinkle evenly with the reserved 1/4 cup cheese and then the bread crumbs. Cut the remaining butter (4 teaspoons) into bits and dot the surface with it. Place

2 tablespoons minced fresh rosemary

1/2 cup half-and-half

3 or 4 medium-large turnips, about 2 pounds in all

1 pound sausage such as Italian-style turkey, pork, or chicken with rosemary

2 tablespoons butter

1 teaspoon salt

1 teaspoon freshly ground black pepper

1 cup grated or shredded Gruyère or other Swiss-style cheese (1/4 pound)

1/4 cup fine fresh bread crumbs

the pan of half-and-half over medium heat and heat until steam rises off the surface. Pour the half-and-half evenly over the prepared dish.

Cover the dish with aluminum foil and place in the oven. Bake for 30 minutes, then remove the foil. Continue to bake until a browned crust has formed and the turnips are easily cut through with the edge of a metal spoon, 15 to 20 minutes longer. Serve hot, scooping out portions directly from the baking dish.

Lettuce Packets Filled with Fresh Water Chestnuts, Mint Leaves, and Pork

Wrapped and rolled to fit into your hand, full of the taste of the hot-off-the-stove spicy filling, and mellowed by cool, sweet bits of water chestnut, these quick and easy-to-prepare packets served with fragrant steamed jasmine rice can be a full meal—if you can make enough of them! These fragrant packets will also serve four as an appetizer.

MAKES 12 ROLLS; SERVES 2

1 head iceberg or other large, sturdy-leaved
   lettuce

12 fresh water chestnuts

1/2 dried red chili such as Anaheim or, for
   more heat, 2 small dried bird's eye chilies

2 garlic cloves, bruised

1 pound ground pork, crumbled into small
   pieces

2-inch square fresh ginger, peeled and minced

1/2 cup fresh chopped or small whole mint
   leaves

1/2 cup rice wine vinegar, plus vinegar for
   serving (optional)

Separate 12 large leaves from the lettuce head and set them aside. Reserve the remainder of the lettuce for another use. With a paring knife, peel away the hard, dark shell-like skin of the water chestnuts, then thinly slice them. Set aside.

Remove the seeds and stems from the chili(es). Put the chili(es) and garlic in a skillet and add the pork. Place over medium heat, and cook, turning occasionally, until the pork is cooked through, about 5 minutes. Discard the garlic and chili(es) and, using a slotted spoon, transfer the pork to absorbent towels or paper to drain.

Place approximately 2 tablespoons of the warm pork mixture on the lower half of each lettuce leaf. Top with about 1 teaspoon water chestnut slices (equal to about 1 water chestnut), several pieces of ginger, a sprinkling of mint, and 1 teaspoon rice wine vinegar. Form each packet by folding the stem end of the leaf up over the filling, then folding in first one side and then another, and finally bringing the upper half of the leaf down, envelope style. Serve immediately while the filling is still warm, with additional rice wine vinegar, if desired.

Poblano Chilies Filled with Radish, Green Onion, Lox, and Teleme Cheese

SERVES 2

Radishes, green onions, and poblano chilies are typically found in the Mexican pantry, but lox and teleme cheese are not. Cooked just long enough to melt the cheese inside the chilies, the radishes and green onions emerge still crunchy and full of fresh taste, while the lox adds dots of bright color and a sophisticated salt undertone. Greek-style black olives can be substituted for the lox if a vegetarian dish is preferred. These chilies also make a good first course, in which case the recipe will serve four.

4 fresh poblano chilies

3 ounces teleme cheese, cut into thin slices

8 large red radishes, minced (about 1/2 cup)

8 green onions, including tender greens, minced (about 1 cup)

1 teaspoon vegetable oil

1/4 cup chopped lox

1/3 cup *crema* (Mexican sour cream), or 1/3 cup regular or light sour cream thinned with 2 tablespoons half-and-half

2/3 cup chopped fresh cilantro

Preheat a broiler or prepare a charcoal or gas grill. Place the chilies on a broiler pan or the grill rack and broil or grill until the skins are charred and blistered, 2 to 3 minutes on each side. Place the chilies in a plastic bag or wrap them in a towel to sweat for about 5 minutes. Using your fingers, peel off the skins. Cut a lengthwise slit in the chili and remove the seeds, but leave the stem intact. Rinse and pat dry. Divide the cheese evenly among the 4 chilies, slipping the slices into the chilies through the slits. Sprinkle about 1 tablespoon each radish and green onion onto the cheese in each chili and then scatter one-fourth of the lox on top of each scattering of onion. Pinch the edges of the chilies closed.

In a nonstick skillet over medium heat, warm the vegetable oil. When the oil is hot, place the filled chilies in the skillet and press them with the flat portion of a wooden spoon or spatula. Cook just until the cheese begins to melt, 2 to 3 minutes. Turn and press again, cooking for another 1 minute.

Transfer the chilies to a serving plate and drizzle with the *crema*. Top with the cilantro and the remaining radishes and green onions and serve.

Old-fashioned Chicken Pie with Butter-Biscuit Topping

few dishes utilize so many of winter's roots in such an agreeable and comforting dish as this one. I have used celery root, potato, onion, leeks, and carrots in this version, but often I will add or substitute parsnips, turnips, shallots, a rutabaga or two, or parsley root, depending upon what is in the garden or cellar. The bottom of the biscuit topping soaks up just enough of the juices below to deliver the perfect texture to that first bite.

SERVES 6

To make the broth, put the chicken in a large soup pot and add water to cover by several inches. Add all of the remaining broth ingredients and bring to a boil over medium-high heat. When a boil is reached, skim off any scum from the surface. Then immediately reduce the heat to low, cover, and simmer until the meat slips easily away from a thigh, 45 minutes to 1 hour. Remove the chicken from the broth and set aside. Strain the broth through a fine-mesh sieve, discarding the vegetables and herbs that have rendered their flavor to it. Set aside.

When the chicken is cool enough to handle, remove the meat, discarding the bones and the skin. Cut or tear the meat into large (bigger than bite-sized) pieces. Set aside. Skim the fat from the broth and then taste for salt, adding more if desired. Measure out 3 1/2 cups and set aside. Reserve any remaining broth for another use.

To prepare the filling, using a paring knife, peel the celery root and cut it into 1 1/2 -inch cubes. Melt the butter in a large skillet over medium heat. Add the celery root, carrots, onions, potatoes, and celery stalks and sauté for 3 or 4 minutes. Add the chicken broth, salt, and pepper. Reduce the heat to low and simmer, uncovered, until the potatoes are tender, 15 to 20 minutes. Taste for seasoning, adding more salt and pepper if desired.

In a small bowl, stir the cornstarch into the water to make a paste. Gradually stir the paste into the simmering broth. Continue to stir until the broth thickens. Stir in the reserved chicken meat, the thyme leaves, parsley, and the celery root leaves, if using. Remove from the heat.

Preheat an oven to 450 degrees F.

To make the crust, sift together the 2 cups flour, baking powder, and salt into a large bowl. Stir in the parsley. Using a pastry blender or two knives, cut the butter into the flour

FOR THE BROTH:

1 chicken, about 3 1/2 pounds

3 leeks, including tender greens, cut into
    several pieces

3 carrots, unpeeled, cut into several pieces

3 celery stalks, cut into several pieces

4 fresh parsley sprigs, each 6 inches long

4 fresh sage sprigs, each 6 inches long

4 fresh thyme sprigs, each 6 inches long

3 fresh bay leaves, or 1 dried bay leaf

1 teaspoon salt

INGREDIENTS CONTINUE ON NEXT PAGE

main dishes

FOR THE FILLING:

1 medium-sized celery root, about 3/4 pound

2 tablespoons butter

4 carrots, about 2/3 pound in all, peeled and
    cut into 1-inch pieces

2 white or yellow onions, quartered

5 medium-sized potatoes, any kind, about
    1 1/2 pounds in all, peeled and cut into
    1-inch pieces

3 celery stalks, diced

3 to 3 1/2 cups reserved chicken broth

1 teaspoon salt

1 teaspoon freshly ground black pepper

2 tablespoons cornstarch

1/4 cup water

meat from cooked chicken

1 tablespoon fresh thyme leaves

1/4 cup chopped fresh parsley

1/4 cup chopped celery root tops (optional)

FOR THE CRUST:

2 cups all-purpose flour, plus flour for dusting

1 tablespoon baking powder

3/4 teaspoon salt

1/4 cup minced fresh parsley

1/4 pound butter, chilled, cut into small pieces

2 eggs, beaten

1/2 cup milk

until the mixture forms pea-sized pieces. Make a well in the center and pour the milk and eggs into it. Using a fork, mix the flour into the egg-milk mixture just enough to make a soft, moist dough.

Dust a work surface with flour and pat out the dough out to make a 3-by-12-inch rectangle about 1/2 inch thick. Fold the dough into thirds: Starting with the short side, lay the left-hand third over the middle third, and lay the right-hand third over that. Pat out the dough again into the original rectangle. Now, fold the dough into thirds again, but this time start with a long side. Repeat this process twice, once from the short side and once from the long side, then pat the dough into a 9-by-12-inch rectangle. The repeated folding and patting out creates the layers of flaky, buttery biscuit topping.

Using a slotted spoon, transfer the filling to a 9-by-12-inch baking dish. Pour in enough of the liquid remaining in the pan to cover the chicken and vegetables. Finally, top with the blanket of biscuit dough. Bake until the crust is browned and baked through, 12 to 15 minutes. Serve hot, scooped directly from the baking dish onto plates.

Jerusalem Artichoke, Green Tomato, and Fresh Corn Pie

SERVES 4 TO 6

This is a dish for late summer or early fall when the last tomatoes on the vines are slow to turn red and the Jerusalem artichokes are freshly dug. The acidic taste of the tomatoes and sweet earthiness of the Jerusalem artichokes set off against the spicy mixture of chorizo, peppers, and corn speak of summer's end.

1/3 pound chorizo or other spicy sausage, casing, if any, removed

1/2 onion, any kind, minced

1 red bell or other sweet pepper, seeded and minced

1 fresh chili pepper such as jalapeño, Hungarian wax, or serrano, seeded and minced

2 ears white or yellow sweet corn

1/4 cup all-purpose flour

2 tablespoons yellow cornmeal

1/2 teaspoon salt

1/2 teaspoon freshly ground black pepper

4 or 5 large green tomatoes, chopped (2 1/2 to 3 cups)

1 1/2 tablespoons butter

1 tablespoon vegetable oil

FOR THE TOPPING:

2 tablespoons all-purpose flour

1 teaspoon baking powder

1/2 teaspoon salt

1/2 teaspoon freshly ground black pepper

3/4 cup yellow cornmeal

2 tablespoons minced fresh thyme

2 eggs, beaten

1/2 cup milk

To make the filling, crumble the sausage into a skillet and place over medium heat. Fry, stirring often, until cooked through and somewhat crumbly, about 5 minutes. Using a slotted spoon, transfer to absorbent towels or paper to drain. Pour off most of the fat from the skillet, leaving a scant 1/2 teaspoon—a thin film—in the skillet. Return the skillet to medium heat, add the onion and the sweet and chili peppers, and sauté, stirring often, until the onion is translucent, 3 or 4 minutes. Transfer to a bowl and set aside.

Remove the husks and silks from the corn and discard. Working with 1 ear of corn at a time, hold the ear upright, thicker end down, in a bowl. Using a sharp knife, cut off the kernels, cutting as close to the cob as possible, and set aside, reserving the accumulated juices.

In a bowl, mix together the flour, cornmeal, salt, and black pepper. Add the green tomatoes to the bowl and turn to coat them with the cornmeal mixture.

In a skillet over medium-high heat, melt 1 tablespoon of the butter with the vegetable oil. When the butter foams, remove the tomatoes from the bowl with a slotted spoon and add them to the skillet, discarding the accumulated juices in the bottom of the bowl. Cook until the tomatoes have browned slightly, 3 or 4 minutes. Turn and cook for another 2 or 3 minutes. Using a slotted spoon, remove the tomatoes to a plate and set aside.

Preheat an oven to 425 degrees F. Use the remaining 1/2 tablespoon butter to grease a 1 1/2-quart baking dish.

To make the topping, in a bowl, combine the flour, baking powder, salt, pepper, cornmeal, and thyme. Stir in the eggs and milk and mix just until thoroughly moistened. Set aside.

Add the cooked chorizo to the corn and its accumulated juices and mix well. Then layer the corn-chorizo mixture in the bottom of the prepared baking dish. Sprinkle with the olives, followed by the fried green tomatoes, and then the Jerusalem artichokes. Pour the topping over the top and, using a spatula, spread it evenly across the surface.

Bake until the topping is slightly puffed and cooked through, 15 to 20 minutes. Remove from the oven, cover loosely with aluminum foil, and let stand for 10 to 15 minutes before serving.

To serve, scoop onto plates directly from the baking dish.

1 cup peeled and minced Jerusalem artichokes (about 2 medium)

12 brine-cured black olives such as Kalamata, pitted and coarsely chopped

Daikon Radish, Pork, and Spinach Stir-fry

The daikon radish absorbs the juices from the marinated pork as it cooks, and the addition of the spinach makes this a well-balanced dish to accompany plain steamed rice.

SERVES 3 OR 4

With a vegetable peeler or paring knife, peel the daikon radish, then cut it into small cubes. You should have about 2 cups. Set aside.

In a bowl, mix together the fish sauce, lemon juice, and cayenne pepper to form a marinade. Add the pork and marinate for 15 to 30 minutes.

Place the oil in a wok or large, deep skillet over high heat. When the oil is hot, add the pork mixture and cook, stirring briskly, for about 2 minutes. Add the radish cubes and cook and stir for another 3 or 4 minutes. Then add the spinach and mix well. Continue to toss and cook just until the spinach has wilted but still retains its bright color, 1 to 2 minutes.

Remove from the heat and serve immediately.

1 medium-sized daikon radish, about 3/4 pound

1 teaspoon fish sauce

2 tablespoons fresh lemon juice (from about 1 lemon)

1/4 teaspoon cayenne pepper

1/4 to 1/3 pound lean boneless pork, cut into small pieces

3 tablespoons light oil such as canola

1 bunch spinach, stemmed

Sunday Roast with Winter Roots

One of my fondest childhood food memories is of Sunday roasts, surrounded by glistening onions, carrots, and potatoes speckled with pepper and herbs. The onions, left whole, wilted slightly and developed a golden translucency and meltingly sweet flavor. The carrots became dark orange, a little crisp on the edges. The potatoes, turned in the pan juices by my mother as they cooked, were a lush sienna. Sometimes there were turnips, too, and rutabagas, and only upon careful inspection could these be differentiated from the potatoes. Turnips were less opaque than the potatoes; the rutabagas were more so, and golden colored.

1 beef chuck roast with bone, 2 to 3 inches
   thick, about 6 pounds

1 teaspoon salt

1 tablespoon freshly ground black pepper

2 garlic cloves

1 tablespoon chopped fresh rosemary

1 tablespoon chopped fresh thyme

4 large onions, any kind

4 large carrots, about 1 pound in all

3 medium-sized turnips, about 3/4 pound
   in all

2 medium-sized rutabagas, about 3/4 pound
   in all

4 large potatoes, any kind, about 1 3/4
   pounds in all

fresh rosemary or thyme sprigs for garnish

Preheat an oven to 325 degrees F.

Rub the roast with half of the salt and pepper, the garlic, and half of the chopped rosemary and thyme. Put it in a baking dish or shallow roasting pan large enough to hold all the vegetables as well. Put the roast in the oven and roast uncovered for 1 1/2 hours.

While the roast is cooking, peel the onions but do not cut through the root ends, as they help the onions retain their shape during cooking. Using a vegetable peeler or paring knife, peel the carrots and cut them into 3-inch lengths. Peel the turnips, rutabagas, and potatoes and cut them lengthwise into quarters.

At the end of the first 1 1/2 hours of cooking, tuck the vegetables around the roast, turning them in the pan juices. Sprinkle them with the remaining salt and pepper and return the dish to the oven. Add the remaining rosemary and thyme, and cook for another 1 1/2 hours, turning the vegetables from time to time. The meat is done when it will separate easily with a fork. The vegetables are done when they are easily pierced with the tines of a fork.

To serve, cut the roast into slices 1/2 inch thick and arrange them on a warmed platter. Surround the sliced meat with the vegetables and drizzle with some of the pan juices. Garnish the platter with sprigs of thyme or rosemary.

a heaping platterful of slow-roasted roots, including whole garlic cloves and shallots, makes an impressive main dish. Served with dipping sauces such as garlic-flavored mayonnaise, sesame and soy, and horseradish mustard, plus a salad of mixed greens and loaves of crusty fresh bread, no one will push back from the table dissatisfied.

SERVES 6 TO 8

Preheat an oven to 350 degrees F.

With a vegetable peeler or paring knife, peel the carrots and parsnips. Cut the carrots into 2-inch lengths. Cut the parsnips in half crosswise, separating the tapering root end from the thick upper portion. Cut the upper portion lengthwise into 2 pieces. Cut off all but $1/2$ inch of the greens from the leeks and discard the greens or reserve them for another use such as making soup or broth. Cut the remaining white portion of each leek into 2 pieces. Cut off all but 2 inches of the green onion tops and discard. Set aside the trimmed green onions. Cut away any leaves from the turnips, leaving a $1/2$-inch stub. Trim off any imperfections on the potatoes but do not peel. Peel the shallots, but do not cut off the root ends as they help the shallots to retain their shape during cooking. Peel the red onions but again do not cut off the root ends. Quarter them lengthwise. Separate the garlic heads into cloves; peel the garlic cloves, but leave them whole.

Put the olive oil, salt, pepper, and thyme, rosemary, and winter savory sprigs in a large bowl or shallow baking dish. Add all of the vegetables and turn them until they are well coated with the oil, herbs, salt, and pepper. With a slotted utensil or tongs, remove all of the vegetables, except the green onions, and arrange in a single layer on 2 baking sheets or in a large, shallow roasting pan. The vegetables will caramelize more on the baking sheets. Reserve the oil mixture in the bowl or dish.

Place the vegetables in the oven and roast for 30 minutes. Turn the roots and baste with some of the reserved olive oil mixture, then add the green onions. Continue roasting, turning once or twice and basting with more olive oil if desired, until all of the vegetables are tender and are easily pierced with the tines of a fork, 30 to 45 minutes longer.

Remove from the oven and arrange the roots on a platter. Serve hot or at room temperature.

6 large carrots, about 1$1/2$ pounds in all

6 medium-sized parsnips, about 1$1/2$ pounds in all

6 large leeks

6 green onions

6 red onions, about 2$1/2$ pounds in all

12 small new potatoes, about 1 pound in all

12 small, young turnips, about 1 pound in all

8 shallots

2 heads garlic, enough for 20 cloves

3/4 cup olive oil

2 teaspoons salt

2 tablespoons freshly ground black pepper

8 fresh thyme sprigs, each 6 inches long

8 fresh rosemary sprigs, each 6 inches long

8 fresh winter savory sprigs, each 6 inches long

main dishes

115

Shepherd's Pie

a thick fluff of mashed potatoes covers this skillet-cooked combination of seasoned ground beef, finely chopped roots of many kinds, and mushrooms. Celery and parsley root, carrots, potatoes, onions, leeks, parsnips, turnips, rutabagas, and Jerusalem and Chinese artichokes are all possibilities to combine with the seasoned meat, and even the potato topping can be varied by mashing a little cooked rutabaga, for example, or celery root with the potatoes.

FOR THE POTATO TOPPING:

6 medium-sized potatoes, any kind, about
  2 1/2 pounds in all, peeled and quartered

1/2 cup milk

2 tablespoons butter

1 teaspoon salt

1 teaspoon freshly ground black pepper

1/2 cup finely chopped celery leaves

FOR THE FILLING:

2 tablespoons light oil such as canola

2 carrots, peeled and finely chopped

1 turnip, peeled and finely chopped

3 potatoes, any kind, peeled and diced

8 celery stalks, diced

16 mushrooms, brushed clean and
  quartered

3/4 pound ground beef chuck

1 teaspoon salt

1 teaspoon freshly ground black pepper

2 cups beef broth

3 tablespoons cornstarch

3 tablespoons water

To make the topping, put the quartered potatoes in a large saucepan and add water to cover generously. Bring to a boil over medium-high heat, then reduce the heat to medium and cook, uncovered, until they can be easily pierced with the tines of a fork, about 20 minutes.

While the potatoes are cooking, prepare the filling. In a skillet over medium-high heat, warm the oil. Add the carrots, turnip, diced potatoes, celery, and mushrooms and sauté, stirring constantly, until the vegetables begin to soften, 6 or 7 minutes. With a slotted spoon, remove the vegetables to a bowl and set aside.

Crumble the ground chuck into the same skillet, and cook over medium heat, stirring occasionally, until lightly browned, 6 or 7 minutes. Remove the beef with the slotted spoon and add it to the vegetables. Mix well and season with the salt and pepper.

Drain off any fat from the skillet and return the pan to the heat. Add the beef broth and bring it to a boil, scraping up any browned bits clinging to the pan bottom. In a small dish, stir together the cornstarch and water to form a thin paste. Stir this paste into the broth. Increase the heat to medium-high and bring the broth mixture to a boil. Reduce the heat to low and simmer, stirring, until the sauce thickens, 3 to 4 minutes. Add the reserved vegetables and beef to the pan and simmer over low heat while you finish preparing the potato topping.

Preheat an oven to 350 degrees F.

Return to the topping. Drain the cooked potatoes, reserving 1/4 cup of their cooking liquid, and place in a bowl. Add 1/4 cup of the milk to the bowl and, using a hand masher, the back of a fork, or an electric hand mixer, mash the potatoes. Add the remaining 1/4 cup milk, the reserved 1/4 cup cooking water, 1 tablespoon of the butter, the salt, pepper, and celery leaves. Continue to mash until the lumps are gone and all the ingredients are fully blended.

Spoon the beef-and-vegetable mixture into a 10-by-16-inch baking dish with 2-inch sides, or into a 10-inch round baking dish with 4-inch sides, such as a soufflé dish. (If you have cooked the filling in a cast-iron or other ovenproof skillet, you may leave the filling in it.) Spread the surface of the mixture with the mashed potatoes. Cut the remaining 1 tablespoon butter into bits and dot the potatoes with the butter. Bake just long enough to set the potatoes and brown them lightly, 10 to 15 minutes.

To serve, scoop out portions with a large serving spoon.

Lamb Shanks with Celery and Parsley Roots

during the slow cooking required for the sinewy meat of the shanks, the celery and parsley roots absorb the pan juices and become so soft as to be nearly dissolved, forming a thick, delectable vegetable sauce. A crisp green salad and country bread is all that is needed to complete the meal.

Serves 4

Preheat an oven to 450 degrees F.

With a paring knife, peel the celery root and then cut it into 2-inch cubes. Peel the parsley roots as well and cut them in half lengthwise. Set the roots aside.

Place the lamb shanks in a roasting pan just large enough to hold them and eventually the roots. Place in the oven and roast for 15 minutes, turning once. Remove from the oven and pour off any accumulated fat in the pan. Tuck the celery and parsley roots around the shanks and sprinkle all with the winter savory, thyme, salt, pepper, and garlic.

Reduce the heat to 350 degrees F. Cover the roasting pan with a tight-fitting lid or seal with a sheet of aluminum foil. Cook until the meat of the shanks pulls away easily from the bone and the vegetables have all but dissolved into a thick sauce, $1\frac{1}{2}$ to 2 hours. About every 30 minutes during cooking, remove the pan from the oven, uncover it, and, with a spatula, turn the vegetables and shanks. Add a little water at the same time; as the vegetables absorb the pan juices, they become more likely to stick to the bottom of the pan, and you want to avoid this.

To serve, place the shanks on a warmed platter and accompany with the thickened vegetable sauce.

1 medium-sized celery root, about 3/4 pound

6 parsley roots, about 1/4 pound in all

4 lamb shanks, about 2 pounds in all

2 tablespoons chopped fresh winter savory

1 tablespoon fresh thyme leaves

1 teaspoon salt

1 1/2 teaspoons freshly ground black pepper

2 garlic cloves, minced

about 1 cup water

Whole Roasted Onions

Whole roasted onions are an old-fashioned dish. I have only vague childhood memories of them coming from the oven, with the tops of their sausage-stuffed centers a crunchy brown and the skins a translucent sienna. It is a dish that deserves a revival, especially since today's farmers' markets offer us much the same wealth of seasonal onions from which to choose as our grandparents had. The stuffing here is similar to a sausage–corn bread stuffing for turkey, and the onions would be well partnered with cranberry sauce and mashed potatoes.

SERVES 4 TO 6

6 red, yellow, or white medium-large
   onions, about 1/3 pound each

1 tablespoon butter

1 large tart apple, peeled, cored, and grated

1/2 pound ground pork

2 cups day-old corn bread, crumbled

1/2 teaspoon salt

1 teaspoon freshly ground black pepper

2 tablespoons minced fresh sage

1 tablespoon minced fresh thyme

1 to 2 cups beef broth or water

Peel each onion and cut a 1-inch slice off the stem end. Leave the root end intact as this helps the onion to hold its shape while cooking. Place the onions in a saucepan just large enough to hold them in a single layer and add water to cover. Bring the water to a boil over medium-high heat, cover, and reduce the heat to medium. Parboil the onions until they have begun to soften slightly and the outer layer of skin has become slightly translucent, about 10 minutes. Using a slotted spoon, transfer the onions to a plate to drain and cool. Reserve 1 cup of the hot cooking water. While the onions are cooling, melt the butter in the hot water and keep warm over low heat.

Preheat an oven to 350 degrees F.

When the onions are cool enough to handle, scoop out their centers with the sharp edge of a metal spoon, leaving a shell approximately 1/2 inch thick. Set aside separately the hollowed-out onions and the centers. Place the apple, pork, corn bread, salt, pepper, sage, and thyme in a bowl. Mince half of the onion centers and add them to the bowl; discard the remaining centers or reserve for another use. Pour the warm water with the melted butter over all and mix well. The stuffing should be moist and pasty; if it is a bit dry, add a little of the beef broth or water. Pack each hollowed-out onion with the filling mixture, mounding it as high as you dare. Place the filled onions upright in a single layer in a baking dish just large enough to hold them. Pour enough beef broth or water around them to reach halfway up their sides.

Bake until the stuffing is well browned and has begun to pull away slightly from the edges of the onions and the skins of the onions are tender when pierced with a fork, about 45 minutes. Using a slotted spoon, remove the onions carefully from the broth. Serve hot.

first marinated, then roasted and basted with the sauce, the chicken develops a subtle taste of spicy ginger tamed with smoky tea that endures, even when the chicken is served cold.

SERVES 4 TO 6

Pat the chicken dry and, with a skewer, prick holes throughout the skin into the meat. Rub it all over with 2 of the garlic cloves and 1 tablespoon of the chopped ginger, and then put the garlic and ginger into the cavity of the bird. In a large glass or earthenware bowl, combine the tea, the remaining ginger, the star anise (if using), salt, and 2 tablespoons of the honey, mixing well. Place the chicken in the bowl and turn the bird over to coat evenly. Cover the bowl and put it in the refrigerator for at least 6 hours or for up to 12 hours, turning the chicken over at the midway point.

Preheat an oven to 350 degrees F.

Remove the chicken from the bowl, reserving the tea mixture in the bowl, and pat it dry. Place the chicken in a shallow baking dish or roasting pan and put it, uncovered, in the oven. In a small saucepan, combine 1 cup of the tea mixture with the remaining 2 garlic cloves and 2 tablespoons honey. Place over low heat and stir until the honey dissolves, 1 or 2 minutes.

After the chicken has been cooking for 30 minutes, remove it from the oven and, using a basting brush, baste it thoroughly with the warm tea-honey mixture. Return the chicken to the oven and continue to baste every 10 to 15 minutes with the pan juices and the remaining tea-honey mixture until it is done and the skin has a deep glossy finish, about 1 hour. To test for doneness, pierce the flesh between the thigh and the breast; the juices should run clear.

Remove from the oven, let stand for 5 minutes, and then carve into serving pieces. Arrange the pieces on a platter and serve.

1 chicken, 3 to 3 1/2 pounds

4 large garlic cloves, bruised

6-inch square fresh ginger, peeled and
    coarsely chopped

2 cups brewed strong, smoky black tea,
    cooled to room temperature

2 star anise (optional)

1/2 teaspoon salt

4 tablespoons strong-flavored honey

main dishes

Breads and Sweets

(potatoes)

That roots belong in sweets is evidenced by the popularity of carrot cake and sweet potato pie, two American dessert classics. Both carrots and sweet potatoes have a high sugar content, as do parsnips. Parsnips were more commonly used in sweet dishes earlier in the century than they are now, but they deserve rediscovery. Consider using them as you would carrots, grated into cake batters or fried and sugared like sweet potatoes.

Potatoes, taro, and yuca, although not sweet, are mashed or puréed and then incorporated into sweet or savory batters or doughs to add moisture and texture. They are made into flours to be used in baking as well. Ginger also lacks sweetness, but its spiciness is so complemented by sugar that it has become associated with sweets, particularly in England. Crystallized ginger and candied ginger in syrup are used in cakes, puddings, and ice creams, where they are frequently combined with chocolate, spices, and dried fruits.

Onions, leeks, shallots, and garlic have a substantial sugar content, but because of their volatile allyl sulfide component, they are infrequently used in strictly sweet or dessert dishes. Instead they are used to sweeten savory breads and puddings, and all cook down into luscious confits for spreading atop flat breads or for folding into doughs and batter.

akin to a soufflé or a stuffing, this is a bread to scoop out and serve as a side dish to accompany grilled chops, rib steaks, or roast chicken. It can also serve as the main course of a light lunch or as part of a hearty breakfast. Very young green garlics or shallots could be substituted for the green onions, and any number of tasty morsels, from smoked salmon to salty olives or capers, can be added. • For a light, fluffy pudding, use a chewy country-style bread that has lots of air incorporated into it. For a more compact, denser pudding, use softer bread.

Serves 6

Preheat an oven to 375 degrees F. Using 1 tablespoon of the butter, thoroughly grease a 9-by-12-inch baking dish with $2^{1}/_{2}$- to 3-inch sides, or a round baking dish (a soufflé dish is perfect) about 10 inches in diameter with $2^{1}/_{2}$- to 3-inch sides.

Put the bread in a bowl, breaking up any large pieces. Pour the milk over the top and push the bread down to submerge it. Let stand until softened, even soggy, about 10 minutes.

Remove the bread from the milk, squeezing it as dry as possible. Stir the eggs, salt, and pepper into the milk until blended and set aside. Scatter one-third of the bread in the bottom of the prepared baking dish. Sprinkle the surface with half of the green onions, herbs, and cheese. Top with half of the remaining bread and then all of the remaining green onions, herbs, and cheese. Layer the remaining bread on top. Pour the milk mixture over all, making sure it seeps to the bottom of the baking dish. Cut the remaining 1 tablespoon butter into bits and dot it across the surface of the bread.

Place in the oven and bake until the pudding is puffed and golden and a knife inserted into the center comes out clean, about 40 minutes. Serve hot or warm, scooping directly from the baking dish onto plates.

2 tablespoons butter

6 to 8 slices day-old bread (see headnote)

4 cups milk

3 eggs, beaten

$1/2$ teaspoon salt

1 teaspoon freshly ground black pepper

$1/2$ cup thinly sliced green onions, including tender greens

$1/4$ cup chopped fresh tarragon, chervil, or parsley, or a mixture

$1/2$ to $3/4$ cup grated Gruyère cheese

breads and sweets

Savory Leek Scones

2 leeks

1 teaspoon olive oil

$^1/_2$ tablespoon butter

$2^1/_2$ cups plus 1 tablespoon all-purpose
  flour, plus flour for dusting

$^1/_2$ teaspoon salt

2 teaspoons baking powder

1 tablespoon minced fresh winter savory,
  or 1 teaspoon minced fresh sage

$^1/_2$ teaspoon freshly ground black pepper

$^1/_4$ cup butter

$^3/_4$ cup milk

$^1/_4$ cup plain yogurt

Split open while still warm and spread with butter or topped with slices of cheese, or served with grilled tomatoes and perhaps a slice or two of bacon, these scones make an enticing breakfast or brunch dish. Nearly like biscuits, I also like them for dinner with a spoonful of old-fashioned creamed chicken ladled over them.

Preheat a broiler.

Cut the whites of the leeks and $^1/_2$ inch or so of the tender greens into $^1/_2$-inch-thick rounds to measure about 1 cup. Place them in a bowl and toss them with the olive oil. Arrange in a single layer on a baking sheet and slip into the broiler about 3 inches from the heat source. Broil for 3 or 4 minutes, then turn and broil for another minute or two, or until the leeks have changed color slightly. Remove from the broiler and let cool.

Preheat an oven to 425 degrees F. Grease a baking sheet with the butter and dust it with the 1 tablespoon flour. Shake off any excess flour.

With a sharp knife, mince the cooled leeks. Set aside. Sift together $2^1/_2$ cups flour, salt, and baking powder into a bowl. Stir in the savory or sage and the pepper. Using a pastry blender or 2 knives, cut the butter into the flour mixture. Finish blending the mixture with your fingers, working the dough just until pea-sized balls form. Stir in the leeks. In a pitcher or bowl, mix together the milk and yogurt until smooth. Form a well in the center of the flour mixture and pour in the milk-yogurt mixture. With a spoon, mix the liquid and dry ingredients together sparingly, just until a sticky dough is barely formed.

Dust a work surface with flour and turn out the dough onto it. Dust your hands as well and knead the dough for a minute or two. Using your fingers or a rolling pin, roll or flatten the dough until it is almost 1 inch thick. Using a knife, cut the dough into 8 free-form triangles and place them on the prepared baking sheet.

Bake until a toothpick inserted into the center comes out clean, 15 to 18 minutes. Remove from the oven. Serve hot or at room temperature.

atted flat, the yeasty dough is spread with soft red onions that have been cooked slowly in olive oil and herbs. Rolled jelly-roll fashion into a loaf, the dough is then baked in a bread pan. Sliced into rounds to serve, the spirals of sweet onions are evident.

MAKES 2 LOAVES; ABOUT 20 SLICES

Preheat an oven to 450 degrees F.

Cut the onion in half crosswise. Cut the halves lengthwise into very thin slices. Spread the slices on a baking sheet in a single layer, drizzle them with the olive oil, and then sprinkle with $1/2$ teaspoon of the salt and the pepper. Turn and toss them to make sure they are coated evenly with the oil. Bake, stirring once or twice, until they are translucent and have begun to crisp a bit, about 10 minutes. Remove from the oven and set aside until it is time to assemble the roll.

Place the lukewarm water in a small bowl and sprinkle the yeast and the 1 teaspoon sugar over the surface. Let the yeast mixture stand for about 5 minutes until it becomes foamy.

Meanwhile, pour the milk into a saucepan and place over medium-high heat. When the milk is very hot but not yet boiling, remove it from the heat and stir in the remaining 2 tablespoons sugar and the 2 teaspoons salt. Pour the mixture into a large bowl and let stand until cooled to lukewarm (108 degrees F).

Add the yeast mixture, eggs, and about 3 cups of the flour to the lukewarm milk mixture. Using a wooden spoon, stir until the flour has combined with the liquid to form a sticky mixture. Next, add the oil and 3 more cups of the flour. At this point, start mixing and kneading with your hands. Still working with your hands, mix in another 1 cup of the flour, to make a total of $7^{1}/2$ cups. Gather the dough into a rough ball and place it on a floured work surface. Knead the dough until it is shiny and elastic, working in a little of the remaining $1/2$ cup flour to prevent sticking, if necessary. This will take at least 5 minutes and maybe more.

Shape the dough into a ball and place it in a bowl lightly rubbed with oil, turning the dough to coat all the surfaces evenly with oil. Cover the bowl with a cloth and place it in a

1 large red onion

2 tablespoons olive oil

$2^{1}/2$ teaspoons salt

1 teaspoon freshly ground black pepper

$1/4$ cup lukewarm water (108 degrees F)

2 packages ($2^{1}/2$ teaspoons each) active
   dry yeast

1 teaspoon plus 2 tablespoons sugar

2 cups milk

2 teaspoons salt

2 eggs, lightly beaten

$7^{1}/2$ to 8 cups all-purpose flour

$1/3$ cup light oil such as canola, plus oil for
   bowl and pans

3 tablespoons minced fresh sage or thyme

6 tablespoons unsalted butter, melted

warm spot to rise (the top of a water heater, near a fireplace or wood stove) until nearly doubled in volume, about 45 minutes.

Punch down the dough in the bowl, re-cover, and let rise again until nearly doubled in volume. Then turn out the dough onto a lightly floured surface and divide it into 2 equal portions. Roll out each portion into a 7-by-12-inch rectangle about 3/8 inch thick.

Thoroughly grease two 4-by-10-inch loaf pans with oil. Brush the surface of each rectangle with 2 tablespoons of the melted butter (4 tablespoons in all) and top with half of the onions and then half of the sage or thyme. Starting from a long side, roll up each rectangle jelly-roll fashion and tuck under the ends. Place each roll, seam side down, in a prepared pan. Brush each top with 1 tablespoon of the remaining melted butter and then cover the pans with a cloth. Place in a warm spot to rise until slightly less than doubled in volume, about 20 minutes. Meanwhile, preheat an oven to 375 degrees F.

Bake until the crusts are browned and the edges have just slightly pulled away from the sides of the pans, 35 to 40 minutes. Remove and let stand in the pans on a rack for 10 minutes. Turn out of the pans and cut into 3/4-inch-thick slices. Serve warm.

Potato and Rosemary Focaccia

MAKES ONE 10-BY-12-INCH SHEET; SERVES 8

a double potato flavor imbues this bread because the water used for cooking the potatoes goes into the dough. Flecked throughout with bits of fresh rosemary and topped with well-seasoned potatoes, a piece, warm or room temperature, served with a lusty salad makes a meal. Consider, too, slicing through a square and sandwiching grilled sausage and apples between the pieces, or perhaps roast turkey and cheese.

2 boiling potatoes such as Red Rose or Yellow
   Finn, about 3/4 pound in all
2 1/2 cups water
1 1/2 teaspoons salt
2 packages (2 1/2 teaspoons each) active dry
   yeast
4 1/2 cups all-purpose flour
3/4 cup olive oil
2 tablespoons minced fresh rosemary
1 teaspoon freshly ground black pepper

Peel the potatoes, cut them crosswise into 1/4-inch-thick slices, and place in a saucepan. Add the water and 1/4 teaspoon of the salt and place over medium-high heat. Bring to a boil, reduce the heat to medium, and cook gently just until the potatoes offer scant resistance when pierced with the tip of a knife, 6 to 8 minutes. Using a slotted spoon, remove the potatoes and set aside. Measure out 1 1/2 cups of the cooking water and let cool to about 108 degrees F, or until the water feels warm to the touch when a drop or two is sprinkled on the inside of your wrist. (If you have allowed it to cool more than that, reheat to the proper temperature.)

In a large bowl, sprinkle the yeast over 1/2 cup of the lukewarm potato water. Let stand for about 5 minutes until it becomes foamy. Add 4 cups of the flour, the remaining 1 cup lukewarm potato water, 1/4 cup of the olive oil, 1 teaspoon of the salt, and all but 1 teaspoon of the rosemary. Mix with a wooden spoon, and then with your hands, until a soft, sticky dough forms. Cover the bowl with a damp kitchen towel and place it in a warm spot (the top of a water heater, near a fireplace or wood stove). Let rise until not quite doubled in volume, about 1 1/2 hours.

Punch down the dough and remove it from the bowl, forming it into a loose ball. Using 1/4 cup of the olive oil, coat the sides of a clean bowl, add the ball of dough to it, and turn the ball to coat it evenly with the oil. Cover the bowl with a damp towel and let the dough rise again in a warm spot until nearly doubled in volume, 20 to 30 minutes.

Preheat an oven to 400 degrees F. Using half of the remaining olive oil, coat the bottom and sides of a 12-by-18-inch (or similar-sized) baking sheet. Dust a work surface with the remaining 1/2 cup flour. Turn out the dough onto the work surface, punch it down, and then flatten it out by stretching it with your hands equally from all sides. It should be approximately 10 by 12 inches and $^1/_2$ inch thick. Lay the dough flat in the center of the baking sheet—it will be smaller than the sheet itself—and place the potatoes in a single layer over the surface. Sprinkle the surface with the remaining $^1/_2$ teaspoon salt and 1 teaspoon rosemary and the pepper. Brush the top with the remaining $^1/_4$ cup olive oil.

Bake until the focaccia is golden brown and the potato slices are slightly browned around the edges, about 20 minutes. Remove from the oven and let cool for at least 5 minutes before cutting. Serve hot, warm, or at room temperature, cut into squares, wedges, or thin slices.

Deep-fried Sweet Potatoes with Cinnamon Sugar

Crisp on the outside, moist inside, these versatile treats can be served as a breakfast sweet or for dessert.

MAKES 10 TO 15 SLICES

light oil such as canola for frying

1 large sweet potato, preferably yellow
   fleshed, about 1 pound

1 teaspoon ground cinnamon

1 cup sugar

Using a vegetable peeler or paring knife, peel the sweet potato, then cut it crosswise into $^1/_2$-inch-thick slices.

In a large, heavy-bottomed skillet, pour in oil to a depth of 1 inch. Place over medium-high heat and heat until it almost smokes and bubbles up around a sample piece of sweet potato slipped into it. Using tongs, and working in batches if necessary, place the sweet potatoes in a single layer in the oil and cook for approximately 2 minutes; turn with the tongs and cook on the other side until golden brown, another 1 to 2 minutes. Lower the heat as necessary if the oil gets too hot. Remove with the tongs and place the slices on absorbent towels or paper to drain.

In a small bowl, mix together the cinnamon and the sugar. Before the sweet potato slices have cooled, roll them in the sugar mixture and arrange them on a plate. Serve hot or at room temperature.

Carrot and Persimmon Tea Cake

both persimmons and carrots contribute to making this an especially moist cake not unlike pumpkin cakebread, but with a fluffier texture. The flavors are of spices, a little citrus, and the faintly exotic yet vague fruitiness of the persimmon. The pointed, burnt red-orange Hachiya variety, which is broad-shouldered at the stem end and tapers to a distinct point, is necessary for this recipe; the firm-fleshed Fuyu persimmons are not suitable. This is an adaptation of a recipe given to me by Betty Kimball.

MAKES ONE 9-INCH BUNDT CAKE; 12 SLICES

4 or 5 very ripe, very soft Hachiya persimmons
  (enough to make 1¹/₂ cups purée)

1 teaspoon baking soda

3 or 4 medium-sized carrots

¹/₂ cup plus 1 tablespoon unsalted butter,
  at room temperature

1¹/₂ cups light brown sugar

2 eggs

1 teaspoon vanilla extract

1-inch piece fresh ginger, peeled and
  finely grated

1¹/₂ teaspoons fresh lemon juice

2 cups all-purpose flour

¹/₂ teaspoon salt

¹/₂ teaspoon ground cinnamon

¹/₂ teaspoon ground cloves

¹/₂ teaspoon freshly grated nutmeg

2 teaspoons grated lemon zest

confectioners' sugar for dusting

Preheat an oven to 350 degrees F.

Peel and seed the persimmons and then purée the pulp in a blender or food processor. Strain the puréed pulp through a sieve. Measure out 1¹/₂ cups purée, add the baking soda to it, and set aside. Reserve any remaining purée for another use.

Using a vegetable peeler or paring knife, peel the carrots. On the fine holes of a hand-held grater, grate the carrots to measure 1¹/₂ cups and set aside. Reserve any remaining carrot for another use.

Put the butter in a large bowl. With the back of a wooden spoon, press it against the sides of the bowl to cream it. Add the brown sugar, eggs, vanilla, grated carrots, ginger, lemon juice, and the persimmon mixture, stirring to blend well. Alternatively, in the same order, process the ingredients in a food processor, just long enough to blend them well, and transfer the mixture to a large bowl. Sift together the flour, salt, cinnamon, cloves, and nutmeg directly onto the butter mixture and then stir until thoroughly blended. Stir in the lemon zest and pour the mixture into an ungreased 9-inch bundt pan.

Bake until puffed and brown, the surface springs back when pushed gently with the tip of your finger, and the cake pulls away slightly from the edges of the pan, about 1 hour. Remove the pan from the oven and let the cake cool in the pan on a rack for 10 minutes. Invert the pan onto a rack to unmold the cake; if necessary, first slide a thin-bladed knife around the edge of the pan to loosen the cake sides. Place the cake upright on the rack to cool completely.

When ready to serve, transfer to a serving plate and dust the top with confectioners' sugar.

here, the rich vanilla custard that forms the base of most ice creams is lightly flavored with shredded ginger, to give the dessert an enticing, slightly perfumed flavor. It might be topped with whipped cream and shards of candied espresso beans, or more simply served atop a slice of fresh apple pie or summer melon.

MAKES ABOUT 1 QUART

Combine the cream, milk, and sugar in a saucepan and place over medium heat. Bring to just below a boil, stirring occasionally to dissolve the sugar. Reduce the heat to low.

Put the egg yolks in a bowl and whisk them until blended. Slowly pour about 1 cup of the hot cream mixture into the bowl, whisking continuously. When well blended and smooth, pour the yolk-cream mixture into the saucepan, whisking continuously. Continue to whisk over low heat until the mixture thickens and becomes custardy enough to coat the back of a spoon without dripping off, about 10 minutes. Remove from the heat and stir in the ginger. Let stand until cooled to lukewarm or room temperature.

Pour the custard into an ice cream maker and freeze according to the manufacturer's directions.

2 cups heavy cream

2 cups milk

3/4 cup sugar

4 large or 5 small egg yolks

2-inch square fresh ginger, peeled and grated
(about 3 tablespoons)

The parsnips, like carrots in carrot cake, add moisture, texture, and fluffiness. Although not necessary, freshly ground spices bring an intense aroma and exotic taste to the finished product. Sprinkled with confectioners' sugar, spread with a buttercream frosting, or left plain, this is a cake for teatime, family desserts, or to nibble along with ice cream. This recipe was adapted from one that has been handed down in my husband's family through several generations.

MAKES ONE 9-BY-13-INCH CAKE; SERVES 12

Preheat an oven to 325 degrees F. Using the 1 teaspoon margarine, grease a 9-by-13-inch baking dish.

With a vegetable peeler or paring knife, peel the parsnip. On the fine holes of a hand-held grater, grate the parsnip to measure 1/2 cup. Set aside. Reserve any leftover parsnip for another use.

Combine the flour, baking powder, and baking soda in a large bowl and set aside. Put the sugar, raisins, parsnip, 7 tablespoons margarine, salt, ginger, cloves, cinnamon, and water in a saucepan. Place over medium heat and bring to a boil. Boil for just 1 or 2 minutes until the margarine has melted and the raisins are plumped. Remove from the heat and let stand until cooled to lukewarm. Pour the lukewarm parsnip-raisin mixture into the flour mixture and stir just enough to moisten the dry ingredients; do not overmix. Pour the batter into the prepared baking dish.

Bake until the edges of the cake start to pull away from the sides of the pan and a toothpick inserted into the center comes out clean, 35 to 40 minutes. Remove from the oven and let cool in the dish on a rack or countertop for 10 to 15 minutes before serving. Cut into 3-by-4-inch pieces to serve.

7 tablespoons plus 1 teaspoon margarine

1 medium-sized parsnip

2 cups all-purpose flour

1 teaspoon baking powder

1 teaspoon baking soda

1 cup sugar

1/3 cup raisins

1/2 teaspoon salt

1 teaspoon finely grated fresh ginger

1/4 teaspoon ground cloves, preferably freshly ground

1 teaspoon ground cinnamon, preferably freshly ground

1 cup water

breads and sweets

Carrot and Orange Muffins

MAKES 12 MUFFINS

Sweet carrots and tart-sweet oranges have an affinity for each other that is further highlighted by the addition of raisins or dates, either in salads or, as here, in muffins. Spread and swirled with buttercream, these make dessert cakes; if left plain, they can be breakfast muffins.

butter for greasing tins (optional), plus
   4 tablespoons unsalted butter, melted
   and cooled

1¹/₂ cups all-purpose flour

¹/₂ cup sugar

2 teaspoons baking powder

¹/₂ teaspoon salt

1 teaspoon ground allspice

¹/₂ cup dark raisins or chopped dates

¹/₂ cup chopped pecans (optional)

1 large carrot

¹/₂ cup milk

2 tablespoons finely grated orange zest

1 egg, lightly beaten

1¹/₂ teaspoons fresh orange juice

Preheat an oven to 325 degrees F. Liberally grease 12 standard muffin-tin wells with butter or line them with paper liners.

Sift together the flour, sugar, baking powder, salt, and allspice into a large bowl. Add the raisins or dates and the pecans, if using, and stir them in until they are coated with the flour mixture. Using a vegetable peeler or paring knife, peel the carrot. On the fine holes of a hand-held grater, grate the carrot to measure ¹/₂ cup. Place in a smaller bowl and add the milk, melted butter, orange zest, egg, grated carrot, and orange juice. Stir until well mixed.

Add the milk mixture to the flour mixture and stir together with a fork just until the dry ingredients are moistened. The batter will be lumpy, as it should be. Spoon the batter into the prepared muffin-tin wells, filling them two-thirds full.

Bake until a toothpick inserted into the center of a muffin comes out clean, 15 to 18 minutes. Remove from the oven and let cool in the pan on a rack or countertop. Serve warm or at room temperature.

baked, then puréed and folded into a custard, the sweet potatoes will sink as the flan cooks, giving it an upper topping of surprisingly dense texture once unmolded. Serve warm or at room temperature with something vanilla, such as cookies or ice cream.

MAKES 8 TO 10 SERVINGS

1 large or 2 medium-sized yellow- or
    orange-fleshed sweet potatoes (to yield
    3/4 cup mashed)

1 cup milk

2 cups heavy cream

6 eggs

1/2 cup sugar

1/2 teaspoon salt

1 teaspoon vanilla extract

Preheat an oven to 350 degrees F.

Place the 1 or 2 sweet potatoes in a small baking dish and bake until they are soft to the center when pierced with the tines of a fork, about 50 minutes. Remove from the oven and, when cool enough to handle, peel and then mash with a fork until smooth, or purée in a blender or food processor. You will need 3/4 cup; reserve any remainder for another use. Reduce the oven temperature to 325 degrees F.

Heat the milk and the cream together in a saucepan over medium heat until bubbles form around the edges of the pan. At the same time, put on a kettle of water and bring it to a boil. In a large bowl, beat the eggs lightly. Add the sugar, salt, vanilla, and sweet potato pulp and stir to blend. When the milk-cream mixture is ready, slowly pour it into the egg mixture, stirring continuously until well mixed.

Butter a 10-inch glass, ceramic, or metal pie pan with 1 1/2-inch sides. Place it in a shallow roasting pan. Pour the custard mixture into the pie pan; it should fill nearly to the rim. Pour the boiling water into the roasting pan to reach halfway up the sides of the pie pan.

Bake until a knife inserted into the center comes out clean, 35 to 45 minutes. Remove the flan from the water-filled roasting pan and let it cool to room temperature.

To unmold the flan, slide a thin-bladed knife or spatula around the edge of the pan to loosen it. Invert a shallow serving plate on top of the flan and, holding the flan pan and the serving plate firmly together, invert them. The flan pan will now be on top and should lift off easily. If the flan didn't unmold on the turnover, give the pan a firm shake to encourage it. Cut into wedges to serve.

Fallen Lemon-Ginger Soufflé

Puffing to airy heights in the oven, this delicately flavored soufflé can be scurried to the table before the inevitable fall, or allowed to collapse into a dense, velvety-textured cross between a pudding and a cake that can be served at your leisure, at room temperature or chilled.

3 tablespoons unsalted butter

1 tablespoon plus 1/4 cup granulated sugar

4 eggs, separated, plus 1 egg white

3 tablespoons all-purpose flour

1 tablespoon grated lemon zest

1-inch square fresh ginger, peeled
  and grated

1/2 teaspoon confectioners' sugar (optional)

Preheat an oven to 400 degrees F. Grease a 3-cup soufflé mold with 1/2 tablespoon of the butter; dust the bottom and sides with the 1 tablespoon granulated sugar.

Place the 5 egg whites in a bowl and beat with a whisk or electric mixer until they form stiff peaks, 3 or 4 minutes. Place the egg yolks in a second bowl and beat them until they are well blended. Set the bowls aside.

Place the remaining 2 1/2 tablespoons butter in a heavy-bottomed saucepan large enough to hold the entire soufflé mixture eventually. Place over medium heat and when the butter melts, remove the pan from the heat and whisk in the flour. Return the pan to medium heat and gradually whisk in the milk in a steady stream. Reduce the heat to low and stir until there are no lumps. Stir in the 1/4 cup granulated sugar, lemon zest, and ginger and simmer, stirring frequently, until a sauce forms that is thick enough to coat the back of a spoon, 10 to 15 minutes.

Remove the pan from the heat once again and whisk in the beaten egg yolks until the mixture is smooth and creamy. Stir one-fourth of the beaten egg whites into the yolk mixture to lighten it. Then carefully fold in the remaining egg whites just until no white streaks remain; do not overmix. Spoon the soufflé mixture into the prepared mold, filling it three-fourths full.

Bake for 5 minutes. Reduce the heat to 375 degrees F and continue to bake until the soufflé is puffed and golden brown and a knife or wooden skewer inserted into the center comes out clean, 20 to 25 minutes. Remove from the oven and serve immediately. Or let the soufflé stand for 10 to 15 minutes and it will collapse, then serve it warm, at room temperature, or slightly chilled. Sprinkle it with confectioners' sugar, if you like, just before serving.

ginger

Bibliography

Brennan, Georgeanne, Isaac Cronin, and Charlotte Glenn.
The New American Vegetable Cookbook. Reading, Massachusetts:
Aris Books/Addison-Wesley, 1985.

Fresh Produce A to Z. Menlo Park, California: Sunset Books, 1987.

Hortus Third Dictionary. New York: Macmillan, 1976.

Larcom, Joy. *Oriental Vegetables, The Complete Guide for Garden and Kitchen.*
Tokyo, Japan: Kodansha International, 1991.

————. *The Salad Garden.* New York: The Viking Press, 1984.

Lorenz, Oscar and Donald N. Maynard. *Knott's Handbook for Vegetable Growers.*
Third Edition. New York: John Wiley & Sons, Inc., 1988.

McGee, Harold. *On Food and Cooking.* New York: Scribner's Sons, 1984.

Schery, Robert W. *Plants for Man.* Second Edition.
Englewood Cliffs, New Jersey: Prentice-Hall, Inc., 1972.

Vilmorin-Andrieux, M.M. *The Vegetable Garden.* London, England:
John Murray, 1885; Berkeley, California: Ten Speed Press, 1980.

Table of Equivalents

THE EXACT EQUIVALENTS IN THE FOLLOWING TABLES HAVE BEEN ROUNDED FOR CONVENIENCE.

us/uk

oz=ounce

lb=pound

in=inch

ft=foot

tbl=tablespoon

fl oz=fluid ounce

qt=quart

METRIC

g=gram

kg=kilogram

mm=millimeter

cm=centimeter

ml=milliliter

l=liter

WEIGHTS

US/UK	METRIC
1 oz	30 g
2 oz	60 g
3 oz	90 g
4 oz (^{1}/$_4$ lb)	125 g
5 oz (^{1}/$_3$ lb)	155 g
6 oz	185 g
7 oz	220 g
8 oz (^{1}/$_2$ lb)	250 g
10 oz	315 g
12 oz (^{3}/$_4$ lb)	375 g
14 oz	440 g
16 oz (1 lb)	500 g
1^1/$_2$ lb	750 g
2 lb	1 kg

OVEN TEMPERATURES

FAHRENHEIT	CELSIUS	GAS
250	120	^{1}/$_2$
275	140	1
300	150	2
325	160	3
350	180	4
375	190	5
400	200	6
425	220	7
450	230	8
475	240	9
500	260	10

LIQUIDS

US	METRIC	UK
2 tbl	30 ml	1 fl oz
^{1}/$_4$ cup	60 ml	2 fl oz
^{1}/$_3$ cup	80 ml	3 fl oz
^{1}/$_2$ cup	125 ml	4 fl oz
^{2}/$_3$ cup	160 ml	5 fl oz
^{3}/$_4$ cup	180 ml	6 fl oz
1 cup	250 ml	8 fl oz
1^1/$_2$ cups	375 ml	12 fl oz
2 cups	500 ml	16 fl oz
4 cups/1 qt	1 L	32 fl oz

LENGTH MEASURES

^{1}/$_8$ in	3 mm
^{1}/$_4$ in	6 mm
^{1}/$_2$ in	12 mm
1 in	2.5 cm
2 in	5 cm
3 in	7.5 cm
4 in	10 cm
5 in	13 cm
6 in	15 cm
7 in	18 cm
8 in	20 cm
9 in	23 cm
10 in	25 cm
11 in	28 cm
12 in/1 ft	30 cm